THE POEMS OF GE...

Poetry translated by Margitt Lehbert

INTO ENGLISH

Michael Augustin  *Koslowski*
Sarah Kirsch  *Winter Music*

INTO GERMAN

Elizabeth Bishop  *Die Farben des Kartographen*
Carol Ann Duffy  *Die Bauchrednerpuppe*
Paul Muldoon  *Auf schmalen Pfaden
durch den tiefen Norden*
(with Hans Christian Oeser)
Les Murray  *Ein ganz gewöhnlicher Regenbogen*
Les Murray  *Traumbabwe*
Les Murray  *Heilige Kühe*
Les Murray  *Gedichte, groß wie Photos*

# The Poems of
# GEORG TRAKL

Translated and introduced by
Margitt Lehbert

ANVIL PRESS POETRY

Published in 2007
by Anvil Press Poetry Ltd
Neptune House  70 Royal Hill  London  SE10 8RF
www.anvilpresspoetry.com

This book is published with financial assistance
from Arts Council England

Designed and set in Ehrhardt by Anvil
Printed and bound in England
by Cromwell Press, Trowbridge, Wiltshire

ISBN 978 0 85646 285 6

A catalogue record for this book
is available from the British Library

# CONTENTS

## *Sebastian in a Dream*

### SEBASTIAN IN A DREAM

## AUTUMN OF THE LONELY ONE

## SEVENFOLD SONG OF DEATH

## *Publications in "Der Brenner" 1914–15*

# INTRODUCTION

*In the meantime I have received "Sebastian in a Dream"*
*and have dipped into it a lot: deeply moved, marvelling,*
*divining and perplexed; for one quickly understands that*
*the conditions of this swelling and fading of music were*
*irretrievably singular, like the circumstances from which a*
*dream might arise. I can imagine that even someone close*
*to him experiences these commanding views and insights as*
*if pressed to panes of glass, as one excluded: for Trakl's*
*experience moves as if in mirror images and fills his entire*
*world, which no one can set foot in, like the space in a*
*mirror. (Who can he have been?)*

RAINER MARIA RILKE, 1915

IMAGINE such a life: early and steady drug and alcohol abuse,
a mother more interested in her collections than her children,
a younger sister the only significant woman in his world,
extreme sensitivity, an abject inability to earn a living, isola-
tion, depression and a deep foreboding of coming disaster. All
this in the political and cultural malaise preceding the First
World War.

And yet Trakl's poems are pieces of music, they never
describe or lament a difficult biography. Trakl wrote poetry to
structure the overwhelming flood of impressions that assaulted
him, "all those voices that reality speaks", the "chaos of
rhythms and images". And music was in contrast the "sound-
ing of harmony and melodiousness in a discordant world."
The individual notes from which he composed his poems may
be culled from personal experience as well as his reading, but
they lose all personal dimension and enter the realm of

abstraction we call pure art. As a striking example, the word "sister" occurs sixty times in his collected poems and prose, yet his writing never invites us to imagine a particular person, his own sister. The figure appears like the women in Munch's paintings: a woman in emotional extremes, but reduced, spare, universal. Geographical names too, readily identified as places in Austria – Mirabell Palace and the Mönchsberg in Salzburg, Anif Palace and Hellbrunn Palace with its trick fountains and gardens, the Hohenburg near Innsbruck – remain purely evocative. His friend Ludwig von Ficker described this perception when he wrote of Trakl's poetry that "its gaze had overcome everything temporal in itself."

Trakl confided in his friends that he experienced rare moments of pure happiness when he wrote well. It was as if the "harmony and melodiousness" he worked on could temporarily protect him from a discordant world and his own discordant place in it. Complaining of plagiarism in an early letter to his friend Buschbeck, Trakl describes the method the poet Ullmann had imitated as "... my own pictorial manner, which in the four lines of a stanza forges together four individual images into a single impression." Most early poems fit this description. The later poetry, which developed at an astonishing pace even as his own life broke apart, continues to create a weave of words, but the form loosens and rhyme disappears. In his essay on Trakl, Heidegger argues that all of Trakl's poetry consists of one large poem. The concentration on a few themes and the quick development of his work could perhaps support this view, but really there is little in common between the early ballads and the mature poems of *Sebastian in a Dream*.

Trakl's images of decay, dung and putrefaction were particularly shocking against the dominant aestheticism of the Art Nouveau movement so popular at the time. His unprecedented use of ugly words and images in beautifully chiselled texts made it difficult to present his work in most ordinary venues. The use of archetypes, myths and literary figures – the hunter and the deer, the sister, the lonely one, Kaspar Hauser, Raskolnikov's innocent whore Sonya and the converted whore Afra of legend – may have been conventional, but the intense dark feeling at the heart of his poetry was repellent to most of his contemporaries.

Later, perhaps because history had proven his unease justified, Trakl's poems developed an enormous impact on readers of German, and what Trakl saw as Ullmann's plagiarism would not be the last attempt to imitate his work. Efforts to emulate Trakl sounded for the most part so much like bad versions of Trakl that a verb was coined to describe the sad result: "es traklt in diesem Gedicht", "it's trakling in this poem", as though for it "to trakl" in a poem were as natural a phenomenon as for it "to rain" in the garden. It was, of course, no compliment. What Trakl had done was, as poets and critics soon agreed, singular.

THE FAMILY of Trakl's mother, Maria Halik, came from Bohemia, that of the father, Tobias Trakl, from the German-speaking population of western Hungary. They met at Maria Halik's wedding in May 1875; Tobias Trakl was best man to the groom. At the time he was a widower and father to seven-year-old William. In 1878, Maria left her first husband and gave birth to a son, Gustav. Tobias Trakl admitted he was the child's father and Maria converted from Catholicism to the Protestant faith of her husband, allowing her both to divorce and to remarry. The Trakls were wed in August 1878 and moved to Salzburg one year later. Gustav died tragically at the age of two and their second child, another son, was baptized Gustav as well. Although the scandalous background of their union was never mentioned in the Trakl household, William, who was eleven when his half-brother Gustav died, would certainly have told his siblings of the family's dark history. Images in Trakl's poetry such as "A wolf tore the firstborn to pieces" or "Your brother dies in an enchanted land" can be seen as inspired by biographical details, even if their effect in the poems is wholly impersonal. Two sisters, Maria and Hermine, were born in 1882 and 1884, Georg Trakl on 3 February 1887, his brother Friedrich in 1890 and finally in 1891 his sister Margarete, or "Grete", who would play such an important role in his life.

Tobias Trakl was a successful ironmonger, Trakl's mother less a passionate mother than a passionate collector and hoarder of beautiful things. Room after room was put off limits to the children as her collections expanded, and she would often lock herself up with her cherished objects, disappearing for days from her children's lives. Trakl later described her as an opium-eater and a neuropath. In his poetry, the image of the mother is always cold, distant and unhappy. Perhaps the emotional frigidity experienced in those earliest years can help to explain Trakl's aloofness, his persistent loneliness. When Georg Trakl was six, his father's business acumen allowed the family to buy a large five-storey house on Mozartplatz. The ironware shop on the ground floor faced the square, in the back was a small courtyard where Trakl watched the rats he would later use in his poetry.

Thankfully an Alsatian governess, Marie Boring, had joined the family when Trakl was three. Warmhearted and Catholic, she taught the children French and probably introduced Trakl to the poetry of Verlaine and Rimbaud. Later, when he developed a real passion for these poets, Marie's French lessons allowed him to read the originals as well as the German translations available at the time. Like all of his siblings, Trakl was given piano lessons, loving the Russian composers a great deal more than Mozart. Many of his poems mention the sound of music, and elements of musical composition of course characterize all his work. Grete, his beloved sister, was such a talented piano player that she later trained to become a concert pianist, a dream that was never fulfilled.

Trakl had always been shy and introverted, he disliked fast movement and often sought isolation. By his own account, he attempted as a child once to stop a horse, once a train by flinging himself before them, and at the age of five simply walked out into a lake, where he was barely saved from drowning. He remembered this as his first suicide attempt, but as he was so young at the time, this interpretation is questionable. Trakl repeatedly told friends that he had always felt magically attracted to water and claimed he had "noticed nothing about his surroundings until he was 20, except for water." He attended a prestigious Protestant school, unusual in a city where 98% of the population was Catholic, later going to an exclusive Catholic school, where he failed Latin, Greek and Mathematics in 1905. This forced him to leave school one year shy of the "Matura" exams. He had, however, acquired enough schooling to choose pharmacy as a profession. This was a disastrous choice of career for a young man who that same year lamented in a letter to a friend his severe problems with chloroform abuse; he was then eighteen. His brother remembered Trakl rubbing opium juice on his cigarettes while still a boy. Trakl also experimented with ether and other substances and later often consumed dangerous amounts of veronal, a barbiturate that he would intentionally overdose, sometimes sleeping for two days and two nights straight. His interest in water, his drug abuse and finally his death by cocaine overdose indicate a yearning for oceanic feelings of dissolution. Drugs for Trakl were not so much a path to expanded consciousness as a way to dull his extreme senses to find rest, sleep and in the end death.

In September 1905, he began three years of training at the apothecary's shop "Zum weißen Engel" (The White Angel), a prerequisite for the two-year course of study for pharmacy later on. The job was not difficult and left him time to read, write and think. He continued to study the authors his teachers condemned: Ibsen (who was also an apothecary), Dostoyevsky,

Nietzsche, discussing their work with his friend, the writer Gustav Streicher. Trakl had already begun writing poetry and prose pieces while still in school and now spent much of his free time working on texts. Unfortunately former classmates derided his choice of professional training, and his family failed to understand his poetry or in fact to show much sympathy for his literary calling. He did have an ally in his sister Grete: he was the poet, she the pianist. But he introduced her to drugs, thereby laying the foundation for her lifelong and life-threatening abuse and Trakl's profound feelings of guilt.

There is no way to know whether Trakl was ever physically intimate with his younger sister. Grete had been placed in a boarding school at the age of eleven, when Trakl was fifteen. Speculation that their parents were reacting to the disquietingly close relationship between the two can neither be proved nor disproved. Trakl's friend Buschbeck, who much later was intimate with Grete for a short period, categorically denied the possibility of incest, while Ludwig von Ficker claims Grete confided an incestuous relationship to him after Trakl's death. By then she was unbalanced by a broken marriage, a miscarriage, a failed career and years of drug abuse, so there is some reason to doubt her claim. The line "In the park, siblings see each other and shiver", from the poem "Dream of Evil", has been quoted as further proof of incest, but Trakl's poetry is never straightforwardly autobiographical, and an unfullfilled incestuous longing could just as well serve as explanation, as indeed could his reading one of many books on the subject.

From 1905 until 1910, his friendship with Streicher sustained him and expanded his horizons. Streicher, a good deal older, more experienced and better connected, was sufficiently impressed by his talent to arrange for the performance of two short theatre pieces by Trakl at the Salzburg City Theatre. The critiques were devastating, and the nineteen-year-old poet burned this early work. Few clues exist to help reconstruct what they must have been like. Certainly they lacked plot. Although fragments and drafts for new theatre pieces were found after Trakl's death, he published only poetry and prose poems after these early disappointments.

Later, Verlaine's thinking and his biography became of great interest to Trakl, who felt increasingly lost in the world of pre-war Austria. The great Frenchman's myth of a "pure childhood", his flight into intoxication, the love-hate relationship with his mother, his worship of the Virgin Mary, all struck strong chords in Trakl. Trakl repeatedly used the name "Maria" in his poetry, but he was not only following Verlaine: his mother, his older sister, his governess all bore versions of that name. Probably most important to Trakl was Verlaine's idea that one must listen to the music of words instead of their weight and meaning: *de la musique avant tout chose* could have been Trakl's motto equally well.

In 1908, Trakl successfully completed his apprenticeship in pharmacy and first exam. More than just a step in his vocational training, this degree entitled him to a privileged one year of military service as an officer instead of the otherwise mandatory three years required of young Austrian men. Later on that year he moved, reluctantly, to Vienna to complete his education and to report for military training. Vienna, then one of the five largest cities in the world, was an ordeal for Trakl, who must have been exhausted and diminished by the onslaught of impressions with which a large city daily confronts its inhabitants. Eventually he established some contacts with intellectual circles, and he did manage to attend his classes and write in his spare time. But his sensitivity was so great he could not use the telephone, and on the train-trips between Vienna and Salzburg, he was forced to stand in the corridor as he could not bear to sit across from a stranger.

The spring of 1909 was very productive for Trakl. Erhard Buschbeck, convinced of his friend's genius, sent a first collection of poems to Langen-Verlag, which turned the manuscript down. Trakl soon renounced the collection. He was an obsessive reviser and took enormous pains with the selection and order of poems in his books. It would be several years before the first one was finished to his satisfaction and printed.

Trakl's father died in June 1910, leaving the family in an unexpectedly precarious financial position. To everyone's surprise, the business was deeply in debt, and Trakl's mother alone inherited the house. Financial worries began haunting Trakl now and would continue to haunt him for the rest of his life. A few weeks after his father's death, Trakl passed his exams without distinction, thus completing his formal education as pharmacist. At the time, the first years of employment were paid so poorly one had to rely on other sources of financial help to survive them. The family business's decline meant Trakl had to live frugally, renting a tiny room with a window looking out onto a light shaft.

In early 1912, Trakl began his year of mandatory military service in the pharmacy of the garrison hospital in Innsbruck. He despised Innsbruck, where he again could barely afford a tiny room. He found the wine taverns sorely wanting, felt depressed and anxious and viewed himself as an outsider. At least he succeeded in performing his duties at the pharmacy. Deeply unhappy that his profession conflicted constantly with his vocation as poet, he read a great deal, especially by and about Rimbaud. Buschbeck introduced Trakl to the literati around Ludwig von Ficker and their magazine *Der Brenner*. This group provided the recognition the poet so direly needed. From then on, individual poems would appear on a regular basis in *Der Brenner*, and the circle associated with it, Karl Borromaeus Heinrich, Karl Röck, Carl Dallago and especially Ludwig von Ficker himself, later proved invaluable both as friends and supporters. They arranged what few readings Trakl gave in his life, but most importantly they took him in when he was too destitute and depressed to cope on his own.

It was apparently during this period that Trakl developed strong religious feelings, claiming at one of the regular

*Brenner*-meetings that the Four Gospels gave mankind more in a few lines than the whole of poetry ever could. Consumed by self-hatred, he declared all poets vain and vanity disgusting. His last aphorism, that "the poem is an incomplete atonement", shows that he had left behind him all influence of Nietzsche. One member of the circle, Karl Röck, noted in his diary that Trakl "wishes for and is convinced he wishes this according to the holy will of God: the increase, the spread, the raging of these destructive illnesses: then people would learn to recognize Our Lord Jesus." Trakl had begun a passionate reading of Kierkegaard, who influenced his thinking greatly. Karl Kraus provided Trakl with a more worldly orientation: they exchanged ideas and written work, and it was Kraus who eventually interested his own publisher in Trakl's poetry.

Having completed his military service in Innsbruck, Trakl apprehensively moved back to Vienna in December 1912. His plan was to work in a government department for pharmaceutical supplies, but after a short attempt to fit in, he quit in a panic and would never again manage to hold a job for more than a few days. His erratic behaviour had discredited him, it became difficult even to get as far as a job interview. Grete had moved to Berlin to study piano, which added to his loneliness. There she agreed to marry her landlady's son, Arthur Lange, who was 34 years older than her and willing to finance her piano studies when her own family was unable to support her. Under the laws of the time, Grete was not old enough yet to marry, and Trakl, who was one of her legal guardians after their father's death, was forced to argue with his mother and half-brother to get them to give their permission for the marriage. Although Arthur was clearly not a suitable match, Grete was declared legally of age and the wedding took place in the summer of 1912.

On 31 December 1912, Trakl was to take the required vow of secrecy for a new position he had managed to find in Vienna. Just one day later, he resigned his new post and for all practical purposes fled to Salzburg the following day. He asked Buschbeck to inform his family of the resignation and to keep his suitcase for him. Trakl then travelled on to Innsbruck, where he stayed in the Villa Hohenburg, which Ficker's younger brother owned. Buschbeck claims this panic-stricken reaction was caused by Trakl's inability to face the room-hunt in Vienna, while Trakl himself explained to Röck that he was too full of his poem "Helian" to carry out regular work. One might add that "Helian" was the poem Trakl was later most satisfied with. The title name is probably a union of Verlaine's "poor Lelian" and the poet Hölderlin, whom Trakl greatly admired.

In April 1913, Kurt Wolff of the Kurt Wolff Verlag in Leipzig wrote to Trakl and asked to buy the rights to a first book of poetry. The press decided to publish a large part of the collection in a series edited by Franz Werfel, who was deeply moved by the poems. When Trakl was informed of this plan, he wrote a vehement telegram refusing permission to print his manuscript in excerpts, announcing he would accept no payment for the book until this issue was resolved. Kurt Wolff quickly agreed to publish the book only as a separate, complete edition. Trakl insisted it appear either in Gothic script or an old form of Roman type, as that would best fit the style of the poems. The book appeared in July 1913 with the simple title *Gedichte* ("Poems"); it was delivered to bookshops in late August to avoid the summer lull in book sales.

Toward the end of his life, contact with Buschbeck seems to have ceased, in all likelihood because of Buschbeck's affair with Grete. Trakl apparently could not forgive him for what he must have seen as a crass breach of friendship. Karl Borromaeus Heinrich, who admired Trakl's poetry and helped him with both public and private praise, also provided Trakl with friendship in that period. Trakl himself was deeply moved by one of Heinrich's novels, in which an incestuous desire, never fullfilled, gives rise to enormous repentance.

But outside poetry, Trakl's life was unravelling. He found it impossible to apply competently for positions and sank into blackest resignation. The family business went irretrievably bankrupt, and although Trakl moved home to help his mother, he soon returned to the Villa Hohenburg, where he lived from April until June 1914. To raise money, Trakl sold off his library. He was working hard on his second book, *Sebastian in a Dream*. His new poems were no longer characterized by four-line stanzas in which each line contained a separate image: instead, he had begun to evolve his own style of free verse. He introduced into his poetry the idea of antiquity as a time of pure humanity, at rest in itself, while he saw contemporary society drifting inexorably towards destruction and decay. Unlike other contemporary poets' work, not one of Trakl's poems is even slightly martial or hymnal. War always remained to him inhumane and terrible. This sensitivity to the calamity of war set him apart from most others, perhaps not least because he showed no real interest in the politics of the day and so was immune to political justifications of the unjustifiable.

An attempt to re-enter the military as a pharmacist failed too. In mid-March, he travelled precipitously to Berlin. Grete had been mentally and physically devastated by a miscarriage. The poet was plagued by dreadful forebodings and helpless despair, but managed with Heinrich, who was also in Berlin at the time, to arrange the poems for *Sebastian in a Dream*. Trakl met the German poet Else Lasker-Schüler in Berlin as well, and they spent hours talking about Christian and Jewish religion, drinking all the while. Both of them apparently had problems with alcohol abuse. Judging from a letter Lasker-Schüler sent Trakl, they had vowed to each other to drink less. But upon his return from Berlin, Trakl had to be helped home from the station. He was so drunk he could not walk unaided.

... in the last few days such terrible things happened that I will not be able to rid myself of their shadow for the rest of my life. Yes, esteemed friend, within a few days my life has been unspeakably broken and what remains is only a speechless pain denied even bitterness.

... It is such a nameless misery when one's world breaks apart. Oh my God, what judgment has come over me. Tell me that I must have the strength to continue living and do the true thing. Tell me that I am not insane. A stony darkness has come over me. Oh my friend, how small and unhappy I have become.

These excerpts are from a letter Trakl sent to his friend Ficker from Berlin. Nobody has been able to determine what actually caused the poet's despair. Speculation includes being told the lost child was his, or that its loss was due to Grete's drug abuse, for which he felt responsible, or that something dreadful happened between him and Heinrich. We shall never know, but one thing is clear: the tensions in Trakl were rising dangerously. In a letter to his future wife, Franz Zeis described the poet as "... a kind man, silent, withdrawn, shy, completely spiritual. Looks strong, powerful, but is actually sensitive, ill. Has hallucinations, is 'barmy' (says Schwab). When he occasionally wishes to express something enigmatic, he has such a tortured manner of speaking, he holds his palms up at shoulder-level, the fingertips raised, clenched, his head slightly tilted, shoulders somewhat raised, his eyes fixed questioningly on you."

By early 1914, Trakl was drinking up to 2½ litres of wine a night, abusing veronal and other drugs regularly and sometimes spending entire days passed out. He drifted from friend to friend, plagued by dreams of suicide, but writing poems from elements he had collected in the past, combining and recombining what seem like musical notes to varying melodies of language. One wife complained of the "large amounts of poison" Trakl was consuming in her home, sleeping until evening every day. What little money the poet had was spent on wine, cigarettes and drugs; there was not nearly enough beyond that to pay for a room and his own food. Writing poetry became a lifeline, a necessity.

Help that Trakl seemed unable to accept came from unexpected quarters. The philosopher Ludwig Wittgenstein had inherited a considerable fortune and decided to distribute a good deal of it to needy artists and writers. He asked his friend Ficker to help him determine promising candidates. 20,000 crowns, enough money to keep him for years, went to Trakl, but he was simply unable to withdraw the money from his account. A friend reported that he saw Trakl fleeing the bank in terror after one of several attempts.

Trakl was still in the reserves as a military pharmacist. When the Austro-Hungarian Empire, antagonistic after the Balkan Wars of 1912–13 and electrified by the assassination of Crown Prince Franz Ferdinand in Sarajevo, declared war on Serbia, he registered for active duty on 5 August. On 28 August, he travelled with his unit to Galicia, arriving on 7 September. After the Battle of Grodek, the first great slaughter of World War I, Trakl attended to over ninety seriously wounded and dying soldiers for two days, all without the aid of a doctor. After a long and harrowing retreat through mud and rain, Trakl and his comrades from Salzburg spent the evenings drinking together. His comrades ridiculed his poems, which upset Trakl greatly, but they seemed to like him personally. When Trakl ran outside one evening, announcing that he felt compelled to shoot himself, they managed to take away his gun in time and Trakl fainted.

After this breakdown, Trakl was transferred to a base hospital in Krakow, from which he attempted to flee and return to the front. Quickly caught, he was imprisoned for four weeks so that his mental state could be observed. Under enormous pressure, Trakl wrote several last poems and letters, but the fear that he would be court-martialled and subsequently executed for cowardice before the enemy allowed him no peace. Practically nothing was done during those weeks to appraise his condition. Ficker managed to visit him in his cell and found him sick with angina, but calm, sharing the cell with his orderly and a man suffering from delirium tremens.

Ficker could not stay for long. Trakl wrote postcards to Wittgenstein and other friends, but no one came to his aid in time. On 2 November 1914, he took an overdose of cocaine and died the next evening. His burial with six others in the Rakovitz cemetery was attended by no priest and no military representative; only his orderly was present. Three days later, Wittgenstein came to visit him and found he was too late. He notified Ficker of the tragedy, who in turn informed Trakl's family.

Eleven years later, Trakl's remains were exhumed and transferred to Austria. On 7 October 1925, he was buried by a Protestant priest and a small congregation of friends and relatives in the cemetery of Mühlau near Innsbruck. Grete could not attend. Drug addiction, alcohol abuse and financial misery had destroyed her life and driven her to suicide in 1917. Of Trakl's five siblings, not one produced offspring; the family died out when his sister Maria passed away in 1973.

## The Translation

AGAINST ALL logic, Trakl's poetry is unusually translatable. He does not, for example, use dialect, slang or historical reference. By remaining universal in his themes he can be quite readily transferred into another language. The difficulty lay in his musicality and his occasional bending of lexical and grammatical norms. I found myself applying strategies I had never used before: making lists of words and the English equivalents I had chosen, changing key words not in a single instance, but in the entire volume, checking the musicality of lines over and over again. It was more like transposing a piece of music for a new instrument. Simple words here evoke complex reactions; rhythms, rhymes and sound patterns create music.

To render this word-music in English, rules were necessary. Rhyming turned out to be impossible; the Trakl in Trakl disappeared in the attempt, making me aware of how carefully he composed the order of his images. Instead I kept, for the most part, the patterns of masculine and feminine endings and the same number of stresses to a line.

Trakl can combine words in a very unconventional manner. "Knospen knistern heiter" is literally "buds crackle serenely". The reader might assume such startling formulations to be a quirk in the translation, but they are equally unusual in German. He constructs words such as "Mönchin", literally "a female monk", from "Mönch" and the feminine ending "-in" which one must render in equally surprising English.

Throughout his poetry, Trakl uses an oddly impersonal way of referring to various figures. He speaks, for example, of "Einsamer" (which I translate as "lonely one"), a grammatically possible but very unusual German noun. Normal usage for a lonely man would be "ein Einsamer", or "ein einsamer Mann". But they sound like someone we might walk up to and befriend. "Einsamer", on the other hand, is a person for whom loneliness is an irremediable part of being.

Trakl's life was short, his œuvre small. It has been the forgivable habit of German editions to collect not just all poems Trakl published, but every version and early draft found in his possession after his death as well. I have chosen to include only the poems which I can be reasonably sure would have come up to Trakl's exacting standards. Early poems he published in magazines and newspapers as a young man, but did not gather into his two first books, are often weak and were left out, while the poems printed after his two books – almost all of them appearing in *Der Brenner* – are included. Probably these poems would have found their way into a third collection we can only speculate about. I hope by this strategy to have produced a collection that would not have set Trakl to sending me furious telegrams.

MARGITT LEHBERT

*Poems*

# THE RAVENS

At noon, across black nooks in haste
The ravens pass with their hard cry.
Past the hind their shadows fly
And then you see them sullenly rest.

O how they mar the brownish calm
In which ploughed fields lie in delight
Like a woman bewitched by growing fright
And now and then you hear them brawl

Over carrion they've sensed somewhere,
And suddenly to the north they'll head
And fade like a procession for the dead
Into the lustful, trembling air.

# THE YOUNG MAID

*Dedicated to Ludwig von Ficker*

### I

By the well, when dusk is falling
You often see her stand enchanted
Drawing water when dusk is falling.
Buckets rise and sink back down.

In the beeches jackdaws flutter
And she looks just like a shadow.
Her yellow hair, her hair will flutter
And the rats will screech in the courtyard.

And caressed by sharp corruption
She lowers now her swollen eyelids.
Withered grass in its corruption
Bends down low before her footsteps.

### 2

She works in silence in the chamber
And the court is long since barren.
In the elder tree before the chamber
A blackbird flutes its plaintive whistle.

Her silver image in the mirror
Regards her weirdly in the twilight

And then fades wanly in the mirror
And she dreads its awful clearness.

A servant sings in dreamlike darkness
And she stares while pain assaults her.
Redness trickles down through darkness.
At the gate the south wind rattles.

3

At night above the barren common
She sways about in feverish dreaming.
A sullen wind cries on the common
And the moon spies from the treetops.

Soon roundabout the stars grow paler
And wearied by their ceaseless labour
Their waxen cheeks grow ever paler.
From the earth decay is seeping.

Reeds are rustling in sad water
And she crouches cold and shivering.
A cock crows far. Across the water
Hard and grey the morning shudders.

4

In the forge there booms a hammer
And she scurries past the doorway.

The servant swings his red-hot hammer
And lifelessly she glances over.

As in a dream she's struck by laughter;
And she sways into the smithy,
Ducking shyly from his laughter
Coarse and brutish like his hammer.

Through the room spray brilliant sparkles
And with short and helpless gestures
She snatches at the vicious sparkles,
To the ground she plunges senseless.


## 5

Stretched out frail upon the mattress
She awakes with sweetest dreading
And she sees her dirty mattress
Draped around with golden shimmer,

The mignonettes tall by the window
And the bluish glowing heavens.
At times the wind brings to the window
The timid chiming of a church-bell.

Shadows glide across the pillow,
Slowly now the noon bells echo.
Her breath is laboured on the pillow,
Like a wound her mouth is open.

## 6

At evening floats the blood-soaked linen,
Clouds hang over silent forests
That are wrapped in blackest linen.
Sparrows clamour on the meadows.

And she lies all white in darkness.
Beneath the roof a cooing murmur.
Like a corpse in shrub and darkness
Round her mouth flies are buzzing.

Dreamlike a sound in brownish waters
Of dance and fiddles reverberates,
Her face is floating through the waters,
Her hair is waving in bare branches.

# NOCTURNAL ROMANCE

Lonely one under a dome of stars
Walks through the silence of midnight.
The boy awakens dazed by dreams,
His grey face crumbling in the moon.

The mad woman cries with loosened hair
By a window staring stiff with bars.
Across the pond two lovers glide
Quite wonderful on their sweet trip.

The murderer smiles pale in the wine,
The sick are seized with fear of death.
The nun is praying bruised and nude
Before Christ's torment on the cross.

The mother softly sings in sleep.
In peace the child regards the night
With eyes that are completely true.
From the whorehouse laughter rings.

By tallow light in the cellar's dark
With his white hand the dead man paints
A grinning silence on the wall.
And the sleeper whispers even now.

## 'AMID RED LEAVES HUNG
## WITH GUITARS'

Amid red leaves hung with guitars
Streams the young girls' yellow hair
By the fence where sunflowers tower.
Through clouds a golden cart moves on.

In the calm of brown shadows, the old
Fall silent in idiot embraces.
Sweetly the orphans sing at vespers.
Flies are buzzing in yellow vapours.

Women do washing at the brook.
The drying linen billows gently.
The young girl who caught my eye
Returns through the dusk of evening.

Sparrows plunge from the tepid sky
Into green holes of putrefaction.
A scent of bread and pungent herbs
Feigns recovery for him who hungers.

# MUSIC IN THE MIRABELL

A fountain sings. The clouds stand
In the clear blue, white and delicate.
In the evening, quiet people walk
Thoughtfully in the ancient garden.

The ancestral marble has turned grey.
A flock of birds fades in the distance.
A faun with deadened eyes looks out
For shadows gliding into darkness.

The leaves fall red from the old tree
And circle in through open windows.
Inside a blush–flame starts to glow
And paint dim ghosts of apprehension.

A white stranger enters the house.
A dog plunges through crumbling hallways.
The maid extinguishes a lamp,
At night one hears sonata–strains.

# MELANCHOLY OF EVENING

– The forest there that spreads deceased –
And shadows surround it, like hedges.
The deer comes trembling from its shelter,
Meanwhile a brook glides by so softly

And follows ferns and ancient boulders
And silvery glints from leafy garlands.
You hear it soon in black abysses –
And maybe stars, perhaps, are shining also.

The gloomy plain seems without measure,
With swamps and ponds and scattered hamlets,
And something feigns a fire's flicker.
A cold shine flits across the roadway.

Along the sky one senses motion,
Whole companies of wild birds wander
To far-off countries, lovely, others.
The reed's small movement sinks and rises.

# WINTER TWILIGHT

*to Max von Esterle*


Pitch-black skies of sheeted metal.
Mad with hunger, crows at evening
Blow across in crimson tempests
Over parkland grieved and pale.

In the clouds a beam congeals;
Then they whirl at Satan's curses
Into a circle sinking downward
Seven of them all in all.

In putrescence sweet and stale,
Silently their beaks are scything.
Houses menace from mute nearness;
Radiance in the playhouse hall.

Churches, bridges, hospital
Grimly stand in fading light.
Blood-flecked linens softly billow
Into sails on the canal.

# RONDEAU

Past and gone the gold of days,
Gone the evening's blue and brown:
The shepherd's flutes sank gently down
Gone the evening's blue and brown
Past and gone the gold of days.

# WOMAN'S BLESSING

Among your women now you stride
And your smile is often troubled:
For such anxious days are coming.
By the fence white poppies wilt.

Swelling lovely like your shape
Grapes ripen to gold on the hillside.
Afar the pond's faint mirror glitters
And in the field the scythe clangs.

In the bushes dewdrops roll,
Reddish leaves are flowing downward.
To come and greet his wife beloved,
A Moor comes to you brown and rough.

# THE BEAUTIFUL CITY

Ancient sunlit squares lie silent.
Deeply spun in gold and azure
Gentle nuns like dreams are rushing,
Under humid beeches silent.

From the brownish glow of churches
Death's pure images are peering,
Lovely shields of mighty princes.
Crowns are gleaming in the churches.

Steeds are rising from the fountain.
Menacing blossom-claws in treetops.
Boys confused by dreams at evening
Play so softly by the fountain.

Maidens stand beside the portals
Shyly watching life's bright colours.
Their moist lips are gently trembling
And they're waiting by the portals.

The shivering chime of bells is sounding,
Marching music rings, and watchmen.
Strangers on the steps are listening.
Organs high in blue are sounding.

Bright-toned instruments are singing.
Through the leafy frames of gardens
Laughter whirrs of lovely ladies.
Softly are young mothers singing.

A fragrance wafts by flowery windows,
Scent of incense, tar and lilac.
Silver-like tired eyelids flicker
Through the flowers by the windows.

# IN AN ABANDONED ROOM

Windows, vivid beds of flowers,
An organ's sound is wafting in.
Shadows dancing on wallpaper,
Whirling madly all around.

All ablaze the bushes waver
And a swarm of gnats will sway.
On distant fields the swish of scything
And an ancient water sings.

Whose breath comes to caress me?
Swallows sketch lunatic signs.
The golden woodland in the distance
Through boundlessness softly flows.

Flames are flickering in the flowers.
This mad dance spins around
Enrapturing, on the yellowed paper.
Through the door someone looks in.

Incense smoke and pears smell sweetly
And glass and chest in twilight doze.
Slow the feverish brow inclines
Down towards the bright white stars.

# TO THE BOY ELIS

Elis, when the blackbird calls in darkest wood,
This is your destruction.
Your lips drink the cool of the blue rock-spring.

When your brow softly bleeds, forsake
Ancient legends
And dark readings of the flight of birds.

But you walk with soft steps into the night
Where purple grapes hang thickly
And you move your arms more gracefully in the blue.

A thorn-bush sounds
Where your moonlike eyes are.
O how long, Elis, have you been deceased.

Your body is a hyacinth
Into which a monk dips his waxen fingers.
Our silence is a black cave

From which at times a gentle beast emerges
And slowly lowers heavy eyelids.
Black dew drips onto your forehead,

The last gold of decayed stars.

# STORMY EVENING

O the deep red hours of evening!
Vine leaves glitter at the window,
Swaying tangled up in blueness,
Inside ghosts of fear are nesting.

Dust sways in the stink of gutters.
At the panes the wind is rattling.
Glaring clouds by lightning driven,
A procession of wild horses.

The pond's mirror loudly shatters.
Gulls are shrieking by the window.
Fire-rider from the hillside charges
Smashed to flames inside the fir wood.

The sick are screaming in the clinic.
Nighttime's plumage buzzes bluish.
All at once a glittering rainfall
Roars its way down to the rooftops.

# EVENING MUSE

The steeple's shadow comes back to the flower window
And something gold. The brow burns up in calm and
    silence.
A well falls in the dark from branches of the chestnut –
Then you sense: it is good! in grievous exhaustion.

The market is bare of all summer fruits and garlands.
The gate's black splendour lends a sense of harmony.
In a garden the notes of gentle play are sounding
Where friends have come to meet after their repast.

The soul will listen gladly to the white magician's stories.
All round, the wheat that reapers cut is softly soughing.
The toilsome life in huts stays mute in patient silence;
The cows' mild sleep inside the shed is lit by lanterns.

Made drunk by breezes, the eyelids soon are sinking
And softly open to the unknown signs of stars above.
Endymion emerges from the dark of ancient oak trees
And bows down low above the mournful waters.

# DREAM OF EVIL

A gong's brown-golden tones are fading –
In black rooms the lover wakes alone,
His cheek at flames that flicker in the window.
On the river, sails, masts, ropes are flashing.

In the throng, a monk, a pregnant woman.
Guitars ring out, red dresses shimmer.
Chestnuts are wasting in the golden shine;
Black the churches' mournful splendour towers.

From pallid masks the soul of evil glances.
A square fades into horrid, gloomy darkness;
At dusk the islands fill with whispers.

A flying bird forms incoherent symbols,
Read by lepers who may decompose by night.
In the park, siblings see each other and shiver.

# SPIRITUAL SONG

A fluttering flower-bed
Paints symbols, rare embroideries.
The deep-blue breath of God flows
Into the garden's halls within,
Serenely in.
A cross looms in the woodbine.

Hear much rejoicing in the village,
Gardeners mowing by the wall,
Softly now an organ plays,
Mixing sound and golden shine,
Sound and shine.
Love shall bless both bread and wine.

Girls are coming in as well
And the cock crows one last time.
Soft a rotten gate swings shut
And in rosary lines of rose,
Lines of rose,
Rests Maria white and fair.

Beggar by the ancient stone
Seems in prayer to have died,
A shepherd softly leaves his hill,
And an angel sings in the grove,
The nearby grove,
Sings the children a lullaby.

# IN AUTUMN

Sunflowers glisten by the fence,
And the sick rest softly in the sun.
In fields the women sing and toil,
The cloister bells begin to peal.

The birds bring you the distant news,
The cloister bells begin to peal.
A violin in the court sounds soft.
Today they're pressing the brown wine.

Cheerful is man then and mild.
Today they're pressing the brown wine.
The chambers of the dead gape wide
Painted lovely by sunshine.

# AT DUSK MY HEART

At dusk you hear the shriek of bats.
Two black horses leap in the meadow.
The red maple rustles.
The traveller chances on the small wayside tavern.
Delicious the taste of nuts and young wine.
Delicious: to stumble drunk into the twilight forest.
Through black branches, the toll of grievous bells.
Dew drips on the face.

# THE PEASANTS

By the window, green and red resound.
In the smoke-blackened, low-ceilinged hall
Farmhands and maids have begun their meal;
And they pour the wine and they break the bread.

In the deep repose of bright midday
Sometimes a scant word is said.
The fields are flickering without pause
And the sky is leaden and wide.

In the stove the embers glow grotesque
And a swarm of flies buzzes and hums.
The maids are listening, foolish and mute,
And blood is hammering at their brows.

And sometimes greedy glances meet
When animal fumes waft through the room.
Dully a farmhand intones the prayer
And a cock crows loud beneath the door.

And back to the field. Dread often takes
Them in the maddening roar of wheat,
And with a clang the scythes swing
Ghostly back and forth in time.

# ALL SOULS' DAY

*To Karl Hauer*

Little men, little women, sad companions,
Today they scatter flowers blue and red
Onto their tombs, which hesitantly brighten.
They act like poor puppets before their death.

O! how fearful they seem and very meek,
Like shadows behind black shrubbery they stand.
On the autumn wind, the cries of the unborn,
You see lights move about in crazy shifts.

The sighs of lovers whisper in the branches,
And mother and child are putrefying there.
The round dance of the living seems unreal
And strangely scattered in the evening wind.

Their lives are confused, full of dim misery.
Take pity, Lord, on these women's hellish pain
And their despondent keening for the dead.
The lonely stroll softly in the hall of stars.

# MELANCHOLY

Bluish shadows. O you dark eyes
That watch me long as I glide by.
The strains of a guitar accompany
The garden's fall, dissolved in brownish lye.
Nymphal hands will now make ready
Death's sombre darkness, withered lips
Suckle at red breasts and in black lye
The sun-youth's humid locks glide by.

## SOUL OF LIFE

Decline that darkens leafy gloom,
Its broad silence within the wood.
Soon a village seems eerily to tilt.
The sister's mouth in black branches whispers.

The lonely one will soon slip away,
Perhaps a shepherd on unlit paths.
From tree arcades an animal steps softly
While its eyelids widen before deity.

The blue river runs splendidly on,
Clouds show themselves at evening;
The soul as well in angelic silence.
Ephemeral creations going down.

# TRANSFIGURED AUTUMN

Immensely does the year thus end
With golden wine and fruit of gardens.
Forests about keep wondrously mute
And are the lonely one's companions.

Then the countryman says: It is good.
You evening bells long and quiet
Provide good heart at the very end.
Migrating birds greet on their journey.

It is the gentle time of love.
In a boat down the blue river
How one lovely image follows another –
This goes down in peace and silence.

# NOOK BY THE FOREST

*To Karl Minnich*


Brown chestnuts. Quietly old people are gliding
Into a stiller evening; lovely leaves softly wither.
By the graveyard, a blackbird jests with the dead cousin,
Angela is accompanied by the fair-haired teacher.

Death's pure images look out from church windows;
But a blood-soaked ground seems very dark and sorrowful.
The gate stays locked today. The key is with the sexton.
In the garden the sister makes kind conversation with ghosts.

In old cellars the wine mellows into gold and clearness.
Apples smell sweet. Joy gleams not very far away.
On a long evening, children love to hear fairy tales;
And often the golden and true show themselves to gentle
    madness.

The blue flows with mignonettes; candles glow within.
For the unassuming, a home is well prepared.
Past the forest's edge a lonely fate is gliding;
Night appears, angel of repose, on the threshold.

# IN WINTER

The tilled field shines white and cold.
The sky is lonely and appalling.
Above the pond the jackdaws circle
And hunters come down from the wood.

A silence lives in black treetops.
A fire's gleam flits from the hovels.
At times far off a sled is ringing
And the grey moon slowly lifts.

A deer bleeds gently by the field's edge
And ravens splash in gory gutters.
The reed quakes tall and yellow.
Frost, smoke, a step in the empty grove.

# INTO AN OLD FAMILY REGISTER

Again and again you return, melancholy,
O gentleness of the lonely soul.
A golden day glows to an end.

Resonant with soft insanity and melodic sound
The patient one humbly submits to pain.
Look! already dusk is falling.

Night returns again and a mortal thing laments
And another feels compassion.

Shuddering beneath autumnal stars
Your head bows lower every year.

# METAMORPHOSIS

Past gardens, autumnal, singed with red:
Here an able life reveals itself in silence.
The hands of man bear the vine's brown harvest,
Meanwhile the gentle pain in his gaze lowers.

In the evening: steps come through black land,
Apparition in the stillness of red beeches.
A blue animal wants to bow before death
And an empty garment horribly decays.

Something tranquil plays before a tavern,
A face has sunk into grass intoxicated.
Elderberries, flutes delicate and drunken,
The scent of mignonettes bathes the feminine.

# SMALL CONCERT

A red that shocks as if you're dreaming –
Through your hands the glow of sunbeams.
You feel your heart insane with pleasure
Preparing softly for a movement.

Yellow fields flow into noontide.
You barely hear the crickets singing,
The reapers' heavy scythe swinging.
Gold woods remain naively quiet.

In greenish pools glows putrefaction.
The fish stand still. God's breathing
Softly wakes a lyre's play in vapour.
To lepers the waters beckon healing.

Daedal's spirit floats in blue shadows,
A scent of milk in the hazel branches.
Long you hear the teacher's fiddle,
The scream of rats in the empty courtyards.

In the tavern on walls with lurid paper
Cooler colours of violets blossom,
Sombre voices died in discord,
Narcissus in the last chord of flutes.

# MANKIND

Mankind lined up in front of fiery chasms,
A drum roll, the brows of sombre warriors,
Footsteps through a fog of blood; black iron chimes,
Despair, night in minds filled with sorrow:
Here Eve's shadow, a hunt and red money.
Clouds shot through by light, the Last Supper.
A soft silence lives in bread and wine,
And twelve in number they are gathered now.
At night they scream in sleep under olive branches;
Saint Thomas dips his hand into a wound's mark.

# THE STROLL

## 1

Music hums in the thicket of afternoon.
In the wheat, sombre scarecrows turn.
Elders softly sway beside the path;
A house glistens to pieces, strange and vague.

In the golden hue hangs a scent of thyme,
A serene number shines there on a rock.
In a meadow, children are playing ball,
Then a tree begins to whirl before you.

A dream: your sister combing her blond hair,
And a far-away friend writes a letter to you.
A hay-rick flees through grey, yellowed and wry
And sometimes wondrous and light you float.

## 2

Time passes by. O sweetest Helios!
O image in the toad-pool sweet and clear;
In the sand, an Eden sinks wondrously.
A bush rocks yellow-hammers in its lap.

Your brother dies in an enchanted land
And your eyes are staring at you like steel.
In the golden hue there a scent of thyme.
A boy sets something near the hamlet on fire.

The lovers in butterflies begin to glow
And swing serenely round number and stone.
Crows take wing from a repulsive meal
And your forehead rages through gentle green.

In the thorn-bush a deer softly dies.
A bright children's day glides after you,
The grey wind that giddily and vague
Washes crumbled scents through the dusk.


3

An ancient lullaby fills you with dread.
By the path a woman piously nurses her child.
Like a sleepwalker you hear her well overflow.
From apple branches falls a consecrated sound.

And bread and wine are sweetened by hard work.
Your hand gropes silvery in search of fruit.
Dead Rachel wanders through the tilled fields.
Green beckons with a gesture full of peace.

Blessed too, the wombs of poor servants bloom,
Who stand there dreaming by the ancient well.
Happily the lonely ones on quiet paths
Walk sinless with the other creatures of God.

# DE PROFUNDIS

It is a stubble field on which a black rain falls.
It is a brown tree that stands alone.
It is a whisper-wind that circles empty huts.
How sad this evening.

Beyond the hamlet
The gentle orphan still gathers scanty ears of wheat.
Her eyes graze round and golden in the twilight
And her womb awaits the bridegroom of heaven.

On their return,
Shepherds found her sweet body
Putrid in the thorn-bush.

A shadow am I, far from gloomy hamlets.
God's silence
I drank from the grove's well.

Cold metal emerges on my brow.
Spiders seek my heart.
It is a light that goes out in my mouth.

At night I found myself upon a heath
Stiff with filth and the dust of stars.
In the hazel-bushes
Crystal angels once more sounded.

# TRUMPETS

Beneath mutilated willows, where brown children play
And leaves drift, trumpets sound. A churchyard shudder.
Flags of scarlet plunge through the maple's sadness,
Riders alongside fields of rye, empty mills.

Or shepherds sing at night and stags enter
The circle of their fires, the grove's ancient sadness,
Dancing figures rise from a black wall;
Flags of scarlet, laughter, madness, trumpets.

# TWILIGHT

In the court, bewitched by milky twilight glow,
Soft invalids glide through things autumn-browned.
Their wax-round gazes ponder golden times
Filled with reveries and peace and wine.

Eerily their sickness seals itself in.
The stars are spreading white melancholy.
In the grey, filled up with deceit and chiming,
See how the horrid scatter in mad haste.

Formless objects of derision, they flit, flutter
And crouch on pathways crossed by blackness.
O! on the walls, shadows filled with sorrow.

The others flee through darkening arcades;
And at night they plunge from red shudders
Of the star wind, like raging maenads.

# SERENE SPRING

### I

By the brook through the yellow unploughed field,
Last year's thin reed still lightly moves.
Wonderful sounds glide through grey,
A scent of warmish dung wafts by.

On willows, catkins dangle gently in the wind,
A dreaming soldier sings his mournful song.
A strip of meadow soughs windswept and frail,
And a child stands in contours soft and mild.

The birches there, the black thorn-bush,
And figures also flee dissolved in smoke.
Things light-green are blooming, others rot
And toads were sleeping through the young leek.

### 2

You I love faithfully, my earthy laundress.
The flood still carries heaven's golden load.
A little fish now flashes by and fades;
Through alders flows a countenance of wax.

In gardens bells sink quietly and long,
A little bird trills like a thing gone mad.
The gentle wheat still and enchanted swells
And even now bees gather with earnest zeal.

Come, love, to the tired labouring man!
Into his hut now falls a tepid ray.
The wood streams over evening harsh and wan
And buds serenely crackle now and then.


3


How everything nascent seems so sick!
A touch of fever circles the village round;
But from branches a gentle spirit waves
And opens up the mind fearful and wide.

A blossoming discharge trickles gently down
And things yet unborn rest in their own peace.
Lovers are blossoming towards their stars
And their breath flows more sweetly through the night.

So painfully true and good it is, what lives;
And softly an ancient stone touches one:
Verily! I will always be with you.
O mouth! that through the silver willow quakes.

# OUTSKIRTS IN THE FÖHN WIND

In the evening the place is bleak and brown,
The air shot through with horrid odours.
From the bridge's arch a train's thunder –
And sparrows flutter over bush and fence.

Crouched huts, paths running to and fro,
In gardens there is disorder and movement,
Sometimes a cry swells from dull emotion,
In a group of children a red dress flies.

A rat-chorus whistles by the waste in love.
Women carry entrails off in baskets,
Slowly they emerge from the twilight,
A revolting train full of dirt and mange.

And a drain suddenly vomits greasy blood
From the slaughterhouse to the quiet river.
The föhn wind tinges meagre shrubs with colour
And slowly red crawls through the flow.

A whisper that drowns in dismal sleep.
Entities sway up from water ditches,
Perhaps as memories of a life completed
That rise and go down with the warm winds.

Avenues emerge shimmering from clouds,
Filled with lovely carriages, bold riders.
Then you see a ship at cliff-sides founder
And from time to time a rose-coloured mosque.

# THE RATS

Into the court the autumnal moon shines white.
From the roof's edge fall fantastic shadows.
In the empty windows a silence dwells;
Then rats appear quietly from below

And scurry whistling back and forth
And a horrid haze of something foul
Wafts after them from the toilet
That ghostly moonlight shudders through

And they squabble in lunatic greed
And fill up the house and barns
That are full of fruit and grain.
Ice-cold winds moan in the dark.

# MELANCHOLY

World-misery ghosts through the afternoon.
Huts flee through gardens brown and bleak.
Shooting lights sway round burnt dung,
Two sleepers reel homeward, grey and vague.

Out on the withered meadow runs a child
And starts playing with its eyes black and smooth.
Gold drips from the bushes dull and weak.
An old man turns sadly in the wind.

In the evening again above my head
Saturn silently rules a wretched fate.
A tree, a dog steps back behind itself
And God's black heaven reels and sheds its leaves.

A little fish glides quickly down the brook;
And gently the dead friend's hand moves
And lovingly smoothes forehead and dress.
A light wakens shadows in the rooms.

# WHISPERED INTO THE AFTERNOON

Sun, autumnally thin and shy,
And fruit falls from the treetops.
Silence lives in blue chambers
For one long afternoon.

The dying sounds of metal ring;
And a white animal collapses.
The rough songs of brown women
Were scattered with the leaves.

The brow dreams colours of God,
Feeling the gentle wings of madness.
Shadows twist upon the hillside
Edged by black putrefaction.

Twilight full of rest and wine:
Sad guitars are trickling.
And to the mild lamp inside
You come as in a dream.

# PSALM

*dedicated to Karl Kraus*


It is a light that the wind has extinguished.
It is a tavern a drunk man leaves before evening.
It is a vineyard, burnt and black with holes full of spiders.
It is a room they have whitewashed with milk.
The madman has died. It is an island in the South Seas
There to receive the sun god. They are beating the drums.
The men perform warlike dances.
The women sway their hips in vines and fiery flowers
When the sea sings. O our lost paradise.


The nymphs have left the golden forests.
The stranger is buried. Then a shimmering rain sets in.
The son of Pan appears in the guise of a navvy
Sleeping the midday hours away by the scorching asphalt.
There are young girls in a yard in smocks of heart-breaking
    need!
There are rooms filled with chords and sonatas.
There are shadows embracing before a tarnished mirror.
Convalescents warm themselves by the windows of the
    clinic.
A white steamer on the canal bears blood-tinged contagion.


The strange sister appears again in someone's evil dreams.
She rests in the hazel-bushes and plays with his stars.
The student, a double perhaps, watches her leave from his
    window.
Behind him his dead brother stands, or he walks down the
    old spiral staircase.

In the dark of brown chestnuts, the young novice's form
    pales.
The garden is inside the evening. Bats fly about in the
    cloister.
The caretaker's children stop playing and search for the sky's
    gold.
A quartet's final chords. The small blind girl runs shivering
    down the lane,
And later her shadow gropes along cold walls, surrounded by
    tales and holy legends.

It is an empty boat that drifts down the black canal in the
    evening.
In the gloom of the old retreat, human ruins decay.
The dead orphans lie beside the garden wall.
From grey rooms, angels with faeces-stained wings emerge.
Worms drip from their yellowed eyelids.
The church square is gloomy and silent as in the days of
    childhood.
Past lives glide by on silver soles
And the shades of the damned descend to the sighing waters.
In his grave, the white magus plays with his snakes.

Above Mount Calvary, God's golden eyes open in silence.

# ROSARY SONGS

## *To His Sister*

Where you pass come fall and evening,
Beneath the trees a blue deer sounds,
This lonely pond of evening.

The flight of birds softly sounds,
Sorrow above your eyebrows' arch.
Your narrow smile sounds.

God bent your eyelids into an arch.
At night the stars, Good Friday's child,
Seek your forehead's arch.

## Proximity of Death

O the evening that enters childhood's gloomy hamlets.
The pond beneath the willows
Fills with the foul sighs of melancholy.

O the forest that softly lowers its brown eyes,
When from the lonely one's bony hands
The purple of his enchanted days sinks down.

O the proximity of death. Let us pray.
Tonight on tepid pillows stained by incense
The frail limbs of lovers dissolve.

## Amen

A putrid thing glides through the rotten room;
Shadows on yellow wallpaper; in dark mirrors
The ivory sadness of our hands forms vaults.

Brown pearls trickle through lifeless fingers.
In the silence
The blue poppy-eyes of an angel open.

The evening too is blue;
The hour of our dying, Azrael's shadow
That darkens a small brown garden.

# DECAY

Evenings, when bells are chiming peace,
I follow the flights of birds in wonder
That long have gathered like pious pilgrims
To vanish in clear autumnal distance.

I stroll through the garden dense with twilight,
And trace their brighter fates while dreaming,
Barely feeling the hour-hand's movement.
Thus over clouds I follow their journeys.

Then a scent of decay makes me shudder.
The blackbird laments in leafless branches.
The red wine sways on rusting fences,

While like the death-dance of pale children
Around dark well-rims worn by weather,
Blue asters in the wind bow low and shiver.

# AT HOME

Into sick windows, a mignonette-scent strays;
An ancient square, chestnuts black and waste.
A golden ray breaks through the roof and flows
Onto the siblings dreamlike and dazed.

Decayed things floating in the slop, the föhn wind
Coos softly in the small brown garden; quietly
The sunflower enjoys its gold and melts away.
In blue air rings the watchman's clattering call.

A mignonette-scent. The walls are drowsing bare.
The sister's sleep is heavy. The night wind delves
Through her hair washed round with lunar glow.

The shadow of a cat glides blue and slim
From rotten roofing hemmed by coming harm,
The purple rearing of a candle's flame.

# AN AUTUMN EVENING

*To Karl Röck*


The brown village. Something dark and striding
Often appears on walls that stand in fall,
Figures: men and women, the deceased go
To cool chambers to prepare the beds.

Here boys play. Heavy shadows spreading
Over pools of brown manure. Maidens go
Through the damp blue and sometimes look
From eyes that are filled with nocturnal chiming.

For lonely things there is a tavern here;
They tarry patiently beneath dark arches,
Cloaked in golden cloud-banks of tobacco.

But always what is yours is black and near.
In ancient arches' shade the drunk man reflects
On flocks of birds that left for distant places.

# HUMAN MISERY

The clock that strikes five before the sun –
A dark dread overwhelms all lonely people,
In the evening garden, bare trees are soughing.
The face of the dead man by the window moves.

Perhaps it's true this hour is standing still.
Before dull eyes, blue images are swaying
To the rhythm of boats that rock on the river.
On the quay a procession of sisters gusts by.

In the hazel, girls are playing pale and blind,
Like lovers who embrace each other while sleeping.
Perhaps round a carcass the flies are singing,
Perhaps a child cries in its mother's womb.

Asters sink down blue and red from hands,
The young man's mouth slips away strange and wisely;
And eyelids flutter quiet and by fear confused;
Through fever's black the smell of bread wafts.

It seems one can even hear a horrid scream;
Through decrepit walls old bones shimmer.
An evil heart laughs loud in lovely chambers;
A dog runs past a man who is in a dream.

An empty coffin loses itself in the dark.
A room will brighten palely for a killer,
While lanterns in nocturnal storms are shattered.
Laurel adorns the noble one's white brow.

# IN THE VILLAGE

### 1

A village emerges from brown walls, a field.
A shepherd decays upon an ancient stone.
The forest's edge encircles animals of blue,
The gentle leaves that into silence fall.

Brown foreheads of peasants. The evening bell
Chimes long; pious custom is a lovely thing,
The Saviour's black head in the bush of thorn,
The cool chamber which death reconciles.

How pale the mothers are. Blue sinks down
Onto the glass and chest they proudly keep;
Also a white head, so old, bends down
Over the grandchild drinking milk and stars.

### 2

The poor man who died lonely in mind
Steps waxen over an ancient path.
The apple trees sink bare and still
Into the colour of their fruit spoiled black.

The roof of meagre straw is arching still
Above the sleep of cows. The blinded maid
Appears in the yard; a blue water laments;
A horse's skull stares from the rotten gate.

With darkened wit the idiot speaks a word
Of love that fades away in the black bush,
Where she stands in her fragile dream-shape.
Evening continues sounding in damp blue.


### 3


Windows slapped by branches the föhn wind tore.
A wild pain grows in the peasant's womb.
Black snow trickles through her arms;
Golden-eyed owls fly around her head.

The walls stare bare and grey-splashed with dirt
Into cool dark. The pregnant body chills
On its fever bed, stared at by a cocky moon.
In front of her chamber a dog has dropped dead.

Three men come in darkly through the gate
With scythes that had been broken in the field.
Through the window clangs red evening wind;
And out of it a black angel appears.

# EVENING SONG

Evenings, when we walk down dark paths,
Our pale shapes appear before us.

When we thirst,
We drink the white waters of the pool,
The sweetness of our sad childhood.

We have died and rest beneath the elders
Watching the grey gulls.

Springtide clouds rise above the gloomy town
That stays mute on the nobler days of monks.

When I took your slender hands
You opened your round eyes softly,
That was long ago.

But when a dark and lovely sound aggrieves the soul,
You, white one, appear in the friend's autumnal landscape.

# THREE GLIMPSES INTO AN OPAL

*To Erhard Buschbeck*


I

Glimpse into opal: a hamlet wreathed by meagre vines,
The silence of grey clouds, yellow hill of boulders
And the cool of evening springs: twin mirrors
Framed by shadows and rocks cloaked with slime.

Autumn's paths and crosses enter eventide,
Singing pilgrims and the blood-stained linen.
The form of the lonely one thus turns inwards
And walks, a pale angel, through the empty grove.

From blackness blows the föhn wind. Slender old women
Consort with satyrs; monks are pale priests of lechery,
Their madness adorns itself with lilies dark and lovely
And lifts its hands to the Godhead's golden shrine.


2

Moistening it, a rose-like drop of dew
Hangs in the rosemary: the scent of graveyard odours,
Of clinics filled with crazy fever-screams and curses.
Bones climb from the family vault putrid and grey.

In blue slime and veils the old man's wife will dance,
Her hair, stiff with dirt, is filled with black teardrops,

The boys have crazy dreams in meagre strands of willow
And leprosy has turned their foreheads bare and rough.

Through the arched window a gentle evening sinks.
From its black stigmatic wounds a saint emerges.
Out of broken shells the purple murex come crawling
And vomit blood on thorny garlands stiff and grey.

### 3

The blind strew incense into festering wounds.
Reddish-gold garments; torches; psalm-singing;
And girls who embrace the Lord's body like poison.
Figures stride stiff as wax through embers and smoke.

A gaunt and bony fool is leading the lepers' dance
At midnight. Garden of peculiar adventures;
Contorted things; grimacing flowers, laughter; monsters
And rolling constellations in the black thorn.

O poverty, beggars' soup, bread and sweet leeks;
This life's daydreams in huts before the forests.
The sky hardens grey above yellow cropland
And after old custom an evening bell sings.

# NIGHT SONG

Breath of the unmoved one. An animal's face
Frozen before blue, blue's holiness.
Immense is the silence within the stone;

The mask of a nocturnal bird. A soft triad of sound
Fades away into one. Elai! your countenance
Leans speechless over bluish waters.

O! you quiet mirrors of truth.
On the ivory brow of the lonely one
Appears the reflected glory of fallen angels.

# HELIAN

In the lonely hours of the mind
It is lovely to walk in the sun
Along the yellow walls of summer.
Soft steps resound in the grass; but the son of Pan
Always sleeps in grey marble.

Evenings on the terrace we got drunk on brown wine.
The peach glows reddish in the leaves;
Gentle sonata, happy laughter.

Lovely is the silence of night.
On a dark plain
We meet ourselves with shepherds and white stars.

When autumn has come
Sober clarity shows itself in the grove.
Calmed now, we stroll along red walls
And our round eyes follow the flight of birds.
In the evening, white water sinks in funeral urns.

The sky celebrates between bare branches.
In his pure hands the peasant carries bread and wine
And fruit ripens peacefully in a sunny chamber.

O how sombre is the countenance of our precious dead.
But the soul is gladdened by an equitable gaze.

*

Immense is the silence of the devastated garden
When the young novice wreathes his brow with brown
    leaves
And his breath drinks icy gold.

Hands touch the age of bluish waters
Or the sister's white cheeks on a cold night.

Quiet and harmonious is a stroll past friendly rooms
Where there is loneliness and the maple's rustle,
Where perhaps the thrush still sings.

Man is beautiful and appears in the dark
When he moves his arms and legs in amazement
And his eyes roll softly in purple sockets.

At vespers the stranger is lost in black November
    destruction,
Beneath rotten branches, past walls filled with leprosy,
Where the holy brother walked long ago,
Absorbed in the gentle lyre-play of his madness,

O how lonely ends the autumn wind.
In dying, the head bows down in the olive tree's darkness.

                    *


Heart-wrenching is the ruin of the lineage.
At this hour the eyes of the one watching
Fill with the gold of his stars.

In the evening, a carillon now silent goes under,
Black walls on the square crumble,
The dead soldier calls to prayer.

A pale angel,
The son steps into the empty house of his fathers.

The sisters have gone far off to white and aged men.
At night the sleeper found them beneath the pillars in
    the hall,
Returned from sad pilgrimages.

O how their hair is stiff with excrement and worms,
When he stands inside with silver feet,
And they emerge dead from bare rooms.

O you psalms in fiery midnight rains,
When servants beat the gentle eyes with nettles,
And the childlike fruit of the elder
Leans over an empty grave, amazed.

Yellowed moons roll softly
Over the young man's fever-linens
Before the silence of winter follows.

                    *


An exalted fate ponders down the valley of Cedron
Where the cedar, a tender creature,
Unfolds beneath the father's blue eyebrows
And a shepherd leads his flock across nocturnal pastures.
Or there are screams in sleep

When a brazen angel approaches man in the grove
And the saint's flesh melts on a glowing grate.

Around clay huts, purple vines sends out their tendrils,
Sounding sheaves of yellowed wheat,
The buzzing of bees, the flight of the crane.
In the evening the resurrected meet on cliff paths.

Lepers are reflected in black waters;
Or weeping they open their excrement-stained robes
To the balsamic wind blowing from the rosy hill.

Slender maidens grope their way through the alleys of
    night,
Hoping to find the loving shepherd.
Saturdays the huts are filled with gentle singing.

Let the song commemorate the boy as well,
His madness and white brows and his demise,
The putrid one who bluishly opens his eyes.
O how sad is this reunion.

                    *

The stages of madness in black rooms,
The shadows of the old beneath the open door.
Then Helian's soul inspects itself in a rosy mirror
And snow and leprosy sink from his forehead.

On the walls the stars have faded
And the white figures of light.

The graves' relics rise from the carpet,
The silence of decayed crosses on the hill,
The sweetness of incense on the purple night wind.

O you broken eyes in black mouths,
When the grandchild gently deranged
In solitude ponders the darker end
And the silent Lord lowers blue eyelids over him.

*Sebastian in a Dream*

*Sebastian in a Dream*

# CHILDHOOD

Full of fruit the elder; childhood lived calmly
In a blue cave. Silent branches ponder
The bygone path where the wild grass sighs
Brownish now; the rustle of leaves

As well, when blue water echoes in the rocks.
Gentle the blackbird's lament. A shepherd
Mutely follows the sun rolling from the autumn hill.

A blue moment is nothing now but soul.
A shy deer emerges from the wood and in the dale
Old bells and gloomy hamlets rest peacefully.

More piously you know the meaning of dark years,
Coolness and autumn in lonely rooms;
And in sacred blue, luminous steps continue to chime.

Softly an open window rattles; tears well up
At the sight of the ruined graveyard on the hill,
The memory of legends told; yet at times the soul brightens
When it remembers joyful people, the dark–gold days of
    spring.

## SONG OF HOURS

With dark glances the lovers regard each other,
The blond, radiant lovers. In bristling gloom
Their frail and longing arms entwine.

The mouths of the blessed broke purple. Their round eyes
Mirror the dark gold of the spring afternoon,
Border and black of forest, twilight fears in the green;
Perhaps the ineffable flight of birds, the path
Of one unborn past gloomy hamlets, lonely summers,
And from ruined blue a decrepit thing at times emerges.

Yellow wheat swishes softly in the field.
Life is hard and the peasant grimly swings his scythe,
The carpenter joins enormous beams.

In autumn leaves turn purple; the monastic spirit
Strolls through serene days; the grape is ripe
And festive the air in spacious courtyards.
Yellowed fruit smells more sweetly; soft is the laughter
Of the joyful one, music and dance in shady cellars;
In the twilight garden, step and silence of the deceased boy.

# ON THE WAY

In the evening they bore the stranger into the chamber of
the dead;
A scent of tar; the quiet rustle of red plane trees;
The dark flight of jackdaws; on the square a guard marched
up.
The sun has sunk into black linen; this evening past keeps
returning.
In the next room, the sister is playing a sonata by Schubert.
Very softly her smile sinks into the crumbling well
Which murmurs bluish in the twilight. O how old is our
lineage.
Someone whispers in the garden below; someone has
deserted this black sky.
On the dresser, fragrant apples. Grandmother lights golden
candles.

O how mild is autumn. In the old park, our steps softly
resound
Beneath tall trees. O how sombre is the hyacinth face of
twilight.
The blue spring at your feet, mysterious the red silence of
your mouth,
Darkened by the slumber of leaves, the dark gold of wilted
sunflowers.
Your eyelids are heavy with poppy and softly dream on my
brow.
Gentle bells tremble through the breast. Your face,
A blue cloud, has sunk onto me in the twilight.
A song accompanies the guitar sounding in a strange tavern,

The wild elderberries there, a November day long ago,
Familiar steps on the twilight stairs, the sight of stained
    beams,
An open window at which sweet hope stayed behind –
All this is inexpressible, O God, we fall to our knees,
    shaken.

O how dark is this night. A purple flame
Went out by my mouth. In the silence
The fearful soul's lonely lyre-play dies.
Permit your head, drunk with wine, to sink into the gutter.

# LANDSCAPE

September evening; dolefully the dark calls of shepherds
    sound
Through the twilight village; fire sparks in the smithy.
A black horse rears immense; the maid's hyacinth curls
Snatch at the ardour of its purple nostrils.
Softly the hind's cry grows rigid at the forest's edge
And the yellow flowers of autumn
Bend mutely over the lake's blue countenance.
In red flame a tree burned down; bats flutter up with dark
    faces.

# TO THE BOY ELIS

Elis, when the blackbird calls in the black wood,
This is your destruction.
Your lips drink the cool of the blue rock-spring.

When your brow gently bleeds, forsake
Ancient legends
And dark readings of the flight of birds.

But you walk with soft steps into the night
Where purple grapes hang thick
And you move your arms more gracefully in the blue.

A thorn-bush sounds
Where your moonlike eyes are.
O how long, Elis, have you been deceased.

Your body is a hyacinth
Into which a monk dips his waxen fingers.
Our silence is a black cave

From which sometimes a gentle beast emerges
And slowly lowers heavy eyelids.
Black dew drips upon your forehead,

The last gold of crumbling stars.

# ELIS

### 1

Perfect is the silence of this golden day.
Beneath old oaks
You appear, Elis, a resting man with round eyes.

Their blueness mirrors the slumber of lovers.
At your mouth
Their rosy sighs fell silent.

In the evening, the fisher pulled up his heavy nets.
A good shepherd
Leads his flock along the forest edge.
O! how just, Elis, are all your days.

Softly the olive tree's
Blue silence sinks along bare walls,
The dark song of an old man fades away.

A golden barge
Rocks, Elis, your heart against the lonely sky.

### 2

A gentle chime of bells sounds in Elis's breast
In the evening,
When his head sinks into the black pillow.

A blue deer
Softly bleeds in the thicket of thorns.

A brown tree stands secluded;
Its blue fruit have fallen away.

Signs and stars
Sink softly into the evening pond.

Behind the hill, winter has come.

Blue doves
At night drink the icy sweat
That runs from Elis's crystal brow.

God's lonely wind
Always sounds by the black walls.

# HOHENBURG

No one is in the house. Autumn in rooms;
Moon-bright sonata
And to awaken at the edge of the twilight forest.

You always think the white visage of man
Far from the turmoil of time;
Green branches bend gladly over something dreaming.

Cross and evening;
The sounding one is enfolded by the purple arms of his
    star
Which rises to uninhabited windows.

This is how the stranger trembles in the dark
When he softly raises his eyelids over something human
Which is far away; the silver voice of the wind in the hall.

# SEBASTIAN IN A DREAM

*for Adolf Loos*


Mother carried the small child in the white moon,
In the shade of the walnut, of the ancient elder,
Drunk with the juice of poppies, the lament of the thrush;
And silently
A bearded face full of pity bent over her

Softly in the window's darkness; and the ancestors'
Old belongings
Lay decaying; love and autumnal dreams.

Equally dark the day of the year, sad childhood,
When the boy softly descended to cool waters, silver fishes,
Calm and countenance;
When he threw himself stonily before seething black horses
And his star came over him in grey night;

Or when he crossed Saint Peter's autumn graveyard
In the evening, holding his mother's ice-cold hand,
A delicate corpse lay silent in the chamber's dark
And raised its cold eyelids over him.

But he was a small bird on bare branches,
The bell long in evening-November,
His father's silence when in sleep he descended the twilight
    spiral stair.

## 2

The soul's peace. Lonely winter evening,
The dark shapes of shepherds by the old pond;
A small child in the straw hut; O how softly
Its face sank away in black fever.
Holy night.

Or when, holding his father's hard hand,
He silently walked up dark Mount Calvary
And in twilight niches of rock
The blue shape of man strode through his legend,
And purple blood ran from a wound beneath the heart.
O how softly the cross rose in the dark soul.

Love; when in black recesses the snow melted,
A blue gust of air played placidly through the old elder,
In the shadowy vault of the walnut;
And the boy's rosy angel appeared softly before him.

Joy; when in cool rooms an evening sonata resounded,
And in brown wooden beams
A blue butterfly crawled from its silver chrysalis.

O the proximity of death. In the stone wall
A yellow head bowed, the child silent,
While that March the moon crumbled.

## 3

Rosy daffodil in the sepulchral vault of night
And the silver voices of the stars,
So that a dark madness sank shuddering from the sleeper's
    brow.

O how quiet a walk down the blue river
Pondering forgotten things while in green branches
The thrush called unfamiliar things into destruction.

Or when, holding the old man's bony hand,
He walked in the evening beyond the crumbling city wall
And the man carried a small rosy child in his black coat,
The spirit of evil appeared in the walnut's shade.

Groping over the green steps of summer. O how softly
The garden withered in the brown silence of autumn,
Scent and melancholy of the old elder,
When in Sebastian's shadow the silver voice of the angel
    died.

# BY THE MOOR

Wayfarer in the black wind; dry reeds whisper softly
In the silence of the moor. Against the grey sky
A flight of wild birds follows;
Diagonals above dark waters.

Commotion. In a crumbling hut
Decay flutters up with black wings;
Crippled birches sigh in the wind.

Evening in a deserted tavern. The way home is scented
By the gentle melancholy of grazing flocks,
Nocturnal apparition: toads surface from silver waters.

# IN SPRING

The snow sank softly beneath dark steps,
In the shade of the tree
Lovers raise their rosy eyelids.

The barge masters' dark cries are forever followed
By star and night;
And the oars quietly keep stroke.

By the crumbling wall, soon violets
Will bloom,
The brow of the lonely one so softly grows green.

# EVENING IN LANS

Journey on foot through twilight summer
Past sheaves of yellowed wheat. Under whitewashed arches
Where the swallow flew in and out, we drank fiery wine.

Lovely: O melancholy and purple laughter.
Evening and the dark scents of green
Cool our burning brows with shudders.

Silver waters trickle over the steps of the forest,
Night, and speechless a forgotten life.
Friend; the leafy footpaths to the village.

# BY THE MÖNCHSBERG

Where in the shade of autumn elms the crumbling path
    descends,
Far from the huts of leaves, the sleeping shepherds,
The dark shape of coolness always follows the wayfarer

Over the footpath of bone, the boy's hyacinth voice
Softly telling the forest's forgotten legend,
Gentler a sick thing now the brother's wild lament.

Thus a sparse green brushes the knee of the stranger,
The petrified head;
Closer the blue spring murmurs the women's lament.

# KASPAR-HAUSER-SONG

*for Bessie Loos*

He truly loved the sun descending purple down the hill,
The paths of the forest, the black singing bird
And the pleasure of green.

Serious was his living in the shade of a tree
And pure his countenance.
God spoke a gentle flame to his heart:
O human!

Softly his step found the town by evening;
The dark lament of his mouth:
I want to be a rider.

But bush followed him and beast,
House and twilight garden of pale people
And his murderer looked for him.

Spring and summer and lovely the autumn
Of the just man, his quiet step
Outside the dark rooms of those dreaming.
At night he remained alone with his star;

Saw that snow fell onto bare branches
And in the twilight hall his murderer's shadow.

The head of the man unborn sank away like silver.

# AT NIGHT

The blue of my eyes has gone out in this night,
The red gold of my heart. O! how softly the light burned,
Your blue coat enfolded the sinking man;
Your red mouth sealed your friend's derangement.

# TRANSFORMATION OF EVIL

Autumn: black striding along the forest's edge; minute of voiceless destruction; the leper's brow listens attentively beneath the bare tree. Evening long past, now sinking across the mossy steps; November. A bell chimes and the shepherd leads a herd of black and red horses into the village. Beneath the hazelnuts, the green hunter is gutting a deer. His hands are steaming with blood and the shade of the animal sighs in the leaves above the man's eyes, brown and silent; the forest. Crows that scatter; three. Their flight resembles a sonata, full of faded chords and masculine dejection; softly a golden cloud disperses. Boys light a fire by the mill. Flame is a brother to the palest and he laughs, buried in his purple hair; or it is a place of murder with a stony path alongside. The barberry bushes have vanished, for years there are dreams in the leaden air beneath pines; fear, green darkness, the gurgle of a drowning man: from the pond of stars, the fisherman pulls a big, black fish, face full of cruelty and madness. The voices of the reeds and of quarrelling men behind him, he rocks in a red barge over freezing autumnal waters, he lives in the dark legends of his lineage and his eyes open like stones above night and virginal horrors. Evil.

What makes you stand still on the crumbling stair in the house of your forefathers? Leaden blackness. What do you lift to your eyes with a silver hand; and your eyelids sink as if drunk with poppy? But through the wall of stone you see the starry sky, the Milky Way, Saturn; red. Raging, the bare tree strikes against the stone wall. You on crumbling steps: tree, star, stone! You, a blue animal that trembles softly;

you, the pale priest who slaughters it by the black altar. O your smile in the dark, sad and evil, to make a child grow pale in his sleep. A red flame sprang from your hand and a moth was burned in it. O the flute of light; O the flute of death. What made you stand still on the crumbling stair in the house of your forefathers? An angel knocks with his crystal finger on the gate below.

O the hell of sleep; dark alley, small brown garden. Softly the shapes of the dead chime in the blue evening. Small green flowers sway around them and their faces have left them. Or their faces bend, faded, over the cold brow of the murderer in the hallway's darkness; adoration, purple flame of lust; dying, the sleeper tripped over black steps into darkness.

Someone left you at the crossroads and you look back a long time. A silver step in the shade of stunted apple trees. The fruit shines purple between black branches and in the grass the snake is casting its skin. O! the dark; the sweat that pearls on the icy brow and the sad dreams in wine, in the village tavern beneath smoke-blackened beams. You, still a wilderness that conjures rosy islands from brown clouds of tobacco, and from within fetches the wild cry of a griffin hunting near black sea-cliffs in storm and ice. You, a green metal and inside a fiery face that wants to go forth and sing from atop the hill of bones of bleak times and the angel's flaming fall. O! despair that collapses with a mute cry.

A dead man visits you. From the heart streams self-spilled blood and on black brows an inexpressible moment nests; dark encounter. You – a purple moon when the other appears in the olive tree's green shade. Followed by never-ending night.

*Autumn of the Lonely One*

# IN THE PARK

Strolling again in the old park,
O! quiet of red and yellow flowers.
You also mourn, you gentle gods,
And the autumnal gold of the elm.
By the bluish pond the reed stands
Still, the thrush falls silent at night.
O! then you too shall bow your head
Before crumbling ancestral marble.

# A WINTER EVENING

When snow falls on the windowpane,
And the evening bell chimes long,
The table is set for many guests
And the house is well stocked up.

Many a journeyer on this way
Arrives by dark paths at the gate.
The tree of grace is blooming gold
Nourished by the earth's cool sap.

The traveller comes quietly in;
Pain has petrified the threshold.
Then on the table in sudden light
The pure gleam of bread and wine.

# THE CURSED

Twilight. Old women come to the well.
In the chestnuts' dark a redness laughs.
From the shop a scent of bread escapes
And sunflowers sink across the fence.

The river tavern still sounds mild and low.
A guitar hums; the clink-chink of coins.
A halo falls upon the waiting girl
By the glass door, sweet and white.

O! the blue gleam she wakens in the panes,
Framed by thorns, black and stiffly rapt.
A stooping scribe is smiling as if mad
Into waters startled by a wild revolt.

2

Evenings the plague hems her blue gown
And a grim guest gently shuts the door.
In the window the maple's black burden sinks;
A boy places his brow in her hand.

Her eyelids often lower heavy and mean.
The child's hands flow through her hair
And his tears stream hot and clear
Into the black empty sockets of her eyes.

A nest of scarlet serpents rears up
Languidly inside her shaken womb.
The arms let go of a thing deceased
That is hemmed round by the sadness of a carpet.


### 3


Into the brown garden a carillon sounds.
Blueness in the dark of chestnuts floats,
The sweet coat of an unfamiliar woman.
Mignonette-scent; and a glowing feel

Of evil. The damp brow bends cold and pale
Over the filth where the rat now roots,
Bathed mildly by the scarlet gleam of stars;
In the garden, apples fall dull and soft.

The night is black. The föhn wind weirdly swells
The white nightdress of the walking boy
And softly the hand of the dead woman gropes
In his mouth. Sonya's smile is fair and mild.

# SONYA

Evening comes to ancient garden;
Sonya's life, blue silence.
Wild birds in long migration;
Bare tree in autumnal silence.

Sunflower, bowing downward
Over Sonya's pale, white life.
Stark red wound, never shown
In dark rooms enables life,

Where the blue bells ring out;
Sonya's step and gentle silence.
A dying beast greets in parting,
Bare tree in autumnal silence.

Sun of the old days shines
Over Sonya's white eyebrows,
Snow that moistens her cheeks,
And the wild of her eyebrows.

# ALONG

Harvested are wheat and grape,
The hamlet in autumnal peace.
Hammer and anvil go on ringing,
Laughter in a purple bower.

Fetch asters from dark fences
For the white young child.
Say how long ago since we died;
Sun wants to appear black.

Small red fish in the pond;
Brow that spies on itself in fear;
Evening breeze at the window soughs,
Blue drone of organs.

Star and secret twinkling
Bids us look up once more.
Mother appears in pain and dread;
Black mignonettes in the dark.

# AUTUMNAL SOUL

Blood-baying and the hunter's call;
Behind cross and the brown hillock
The mirror of the pond dulls softly
And the hawk cries hard and bright.

Above the stubble-field and path
A black silence already trembles;
Pure sky between the branches;
The brook alone runs soft and true.

Soon fish and deer will slide off.
Blue soul and dark wandering
Severed us from loved ones, others.
Evening switches image and sense.

A just life's bread and wine,
God, into your gentle hands
Man places his dark ending,
All red torment and all guilt.

## AFRA

A child with chestnut hair. Prayer and amen
Softly darken the coolness of evening
And Afra's smile, red in a yellow frame
Of sunflowers, fear and grey humidity.

Wrapped in a blue coat, long ago the monk
Saw her piously painted on church windows;
That shall, in pain, still be a kind companion
When his blood is haunted by her stars.

Autumnal ruin; and the silence of the elder.
The brow touches the water's blue movement,
A cloth of hair draped upon a bier.

Rotting fruit falls from the branches;
Inexpressible is the birds' flight, encounter
With the dying; followed by dark years.

# AUTUMN OF THE LONELY ONE

Dark autumn comes full of fruit and plenty,
The faded gleam of lovely summer days.
A pure blue emerges from the ruined shell;
The flight of birds resounds with old legends.
The wine has been pressed, the mild silence
Filled with the quiet reply to dark questions.

And here and there a cross on a barren hill;
In the red forest a herd is disappearing.
The cloud meanders over the pond's mirror;
The calm gesture of the peasant is at rest.
Very softly evening's blue wing touches
A roof of parched straw, the black earth.

Soon stars will nest in the brows of the tired;
A quiet simplicity enters cool chambers
And angels step soundlessly from the blue
Eyes of lovers who are suffering more gently.
The reed murmurs; a bony horror strikes
When black the dew drips down from bare willows.

*Sevenfold Song of Death*

# REST AND SILENCE

Shepherds buried the sun in the barren wood.
A fisherman pulled
The moon from a freezing pond in a net of hair.

Inside the blue crystal
A pale man lives, his cheek leaning against his stars;
Or he lowers his head in purple sleep.

But the black flight of birds always stirs
The one who watches, the holiness of blue flowers,
Close tranquillity thinks of things forgotten, extinguished
    angels.

The brow becomes night again in lunar stone;
A luminous youth
The sister appears in autumn and black decay.

# ANIF

Memory: gulls gliding across the dark sky
Of masculine dejection.
Silently you live in the shadow of the autumn ash,
Absorbed in the just measure of the hill;

You always walk down the green river
When evening has come,
Resounding love; peacefully the dark deer meets,

A rosy man. Drunk with a bluish scent
The brow touches dying leaves
And thinks the sombre face of the mother;
O, how all things sink into the dark;

The austere rooms and old belongings
Of the fathers.
This dismays the stranger's breast.
O, you signs and stars.

Great is the guilt of things born. Woe, you golden shudders
Of death,
When the soul dreams cooler blossoms.

In the bare branches the bird of night is always calling.
Above the steps of the lunar one
An icy wind sounds at the village walls.

# BIRTH

Mountains: blackness, silence and snow.
The hunt descends red from the forest;
O, the mossy glances of the deer.

Silence of the mother; beneath black firs,
Sleeping hands open
When the cold, crumbling moon appears.

O, the birth of man. Nightly blue water
Murmurs in the rocky gorge;
Sighing, the fallen angel sees his image,

Something pale awakes in a musty chamber.
Two moons,
The eyes of the old stone woman light up.

Woe, scream of the woman in labour. Night
With black wing brushes the boy's brow,
Snow that sinks softly from a purple cloud.

# DESTRUCTION

*To Karl Borromaeus Heinrich*


Over the white pond
The wild birds have passed and gone.
In the evening an icy wind blows from our stars.

Over our graves
Bends the broken forehead of night.
Beneath oaks we rock in a silver boat.

The white walls of the city constantly sound.
Beneath an arch of thorn
O my brother we climb blind clock-hands toward midnight.

# TO ONE WHO DIED YOUNG

O, the black angel who emerged quietly from the tree's core,
When in the evening we were gentle playmates
At the rim of the bluish well.
Calm was our step, round eyes in the brown autumnal cool,
O, the purple sweetness of the stars.

But he went down the stone steps of the Mönchsberg,
A blue smile on his face and strangely pupated
Into his more silent childhood, and died;
And in the garden the friend's silver face lingered,
Listening in the leaves or the old stones.

Soul sang death, the green putrefaction of flesh
And it was the rustle of the forest,
The fervent lament of the deer.
From twilight towers, the blue bells of evening always
      sounded.

The hour came when he saw shadows in the purple sun,
Shadows of decay in bare branches;
Evening, when the blackbird sang near the twilight wall,
The spirit of the one who died young softly entered the
      room.

O, the blood that flows from the resounding throat,
Blue flower; O the fiery tear
Cried into the night.

Golden cloud and time. In the lonely chamber
You often invite the dead man
And stroll down the green river conversing beneath elms.

# SPIRITUAL TWILIGHT

Quietly a dark deer encounters
At the edge of the wood;
By the hill the evening wind softly ends,

The blackbird's lament falls silent
And the gentle flutes of autumn
Are soundless in the reeds.

On a black cloud
You ride, drunk with poppy,
On the nightly pond,

The starry sky.
Ever the sister's lunar voice sounds
Through the spiritual night.

# OCCIDENTAL SONG

O the nocturnal wing-beat of the soul:
Shepherds, we once walked along the twilight forest
And the red deer, green flower and slurring spring
Followed humbly. O, the ancient call of the house cricket,
Blood blossoming by the sacrificial stone
And the cry of a lonely bird above the pond's green silence.

O, you crusades and burning torments
Of the flesh, the fall of purple fruit
In the evening garden where pious disciples walked long ago,
Warriors now, waking from their wounds and star-dreams.
O, the cyan cornflower-bundle of night.

O, you times of silence and golden autumns,
When we peaceful monks pressed the purple grape;
And all around hill and forest gleamed.
O, you hunts and castles; repose of evening,
When man in his chamber dwelled on righteous thoughts,
In silent prayer wrestled for God's living head.

O, the bitter hour of destruction,
When we gaze upon a face of stone in black waters.
But shining, lovers raise their silver eyelids:
*One* lineage. Incense streams from rosy pillows
And the sweet song of the resurrected.

# TRANSFIGURATION

When evening comes,
A blue countenance softly leaves you.
A small bird sings in the tamarind tree.

A gentle monk
Folds his lifeless hands.
A white angel visits Mary.

A nightly wreath
Of violets, wheat and purple grapes
Is the year of the one who watches.

At your feet
The graves of the dead open
When you lay your brow into your silver hands.

The autumnal moon
Lives silently at your mouth,
Dark song drunk with poppy juice;

Blue flower
Softly sounding in the yellowed stone.

# FÖHN WIND

Blind lament in the wind, moonlike winter days,
Childhood, footsteps fade softly by the black hedge,
The long chime of evening bells.
Softly white night draws near,

Transforms the pain and labour of a stony life
Into purple dreams
So the thorny sting will never leave off the decaying body.

Deep in its slumber, the fearful soul sighs,

Deep the wind in broken trees,
And the mourning form of the mother
Reels through the lonely forest

Of this mute sadness; nights
Filled with tears, fiery angels.
A child's skeleton shatters silver against the bare wall.

# THE WAYFARER

White night forever leans against the hill
Where the poplar looms in silver sounds,
Where stars exist and stones.

Sleeping, a footbridge arches across the torrent,
The boy is followed by a lifeless face,
Crescent moon in a rosy gorge

Far from praising shepherds. Between old rocks
The toad peers from crystal eyes,
The blossoming wind awakens, bird-voice of the deathlike
    one
And the steps grow softly green in the forest.

This recalls tree and animal. Slow stairs of moss;
And the moon
Sinking radiant into sad waters.

He returns and strolls by the green shore,
Rocks through the crumbling city in a small black gondola.

# KARL KRAUS

White high priest of truth,
Crystal voice in which God's icy breath dwells,
Angry magus
Under whose blazing coat the warrior's blue armour clinks.

# TO THE ONES WHO FELL SILENT

O, the madness of the big city, when in the evening
Stunted trees jut up by the black wall
And the spirit of evil watches from its silver mask;
Light with a magnetic lash drives out the stony night.
O, the sunken chime of evening bells.

A whore who with icy shudders gives birth to a small dead
    child.
Raging, God's wrath whips the brow of the one possessed,
Purple scourge, hunger that shatters green eyes.
O, the gruesome laughter of gold.

But in a dark cave, a muter mankind silently bleeds
And from hard metals assembles the redeeming head.

# PASSION

When Orpheus strikes the silvery lute,
Mourning something dead in the evening garden,
Who are you, thing resting beneath tall trees?
Autumnal reeds rustle laments,
The blue pond
Dying slowly beneath greening trees
And following the sister's shadow;
Dark love
Of a savage lineage
Which day flees from on golden wheels.
Silent night.

Beneath gloomy firs
Two wolves mingled their blood
In a stony embrace; a thing of gold
The cloud dispersed above the path,
Patience and silence of childhood.
Again the delicate corpse meets
At the pond of Triton
Slumbering in its hyacinth hair.
If but the cool head would finally shatter!

For always a blue deer, watchful beast,
Follows beneath twilight trees, vigilant
Along these darker paths
And moved by nightly melodious sound,
Gentle madness;

Or the lute sounded
Full of dark enchantment
At the cool feet of the penitent
In the city of stone.

# SEVENFOLD SONG OF DEATH

Spring dawns in shades of blue; beneath drinking trees
A dark thing strolls in evening and destruction,
Listening to the blackbird's gentle lament.
Silently night appears, a bleeding deer
That slowly sinks away on the hillside.

In the moist air, blooming apple-branches sway,
What is entwined comes silvery undone,
Dying out of nightly eyes; falling stars;
Gentle singing of childhood.

As one appearing, the sleeper went down the black forest
And a blue spring murmured in the vale
So that he softly raised pale eyelids
Above his snowy countenance;

And the moon chased a red animal
From its cave;
And in sighs the dark lament of the women died.

The white stranger raised his hands more radiantly
To his star;
Mutely a dead thing leaves the crumbling house.

O man's putrid form: forged from cold metals,
Night and dread of sunken forests
And the animal's scorching wildness;
Windless calm of the soul.

On a blackish barge he floated down shimmering streams,
Full of purple stars, and greening branches
Sank peacefully down on him,
Poppy from a silver cloud.

# WINTER NIGHT

Snow has fallen. Drunk on purple wine, you leave the dark district of man, the red flame of his hearth, after midnight. O this darkness!

Black frost. The earth is hard, the air tastes of bitter things. Your stars assemble into evil omens.

With steps of stone you plod along the tracks, with round eyes, like a soldier storming a black bulwark. Avanti!

Bitter snow and moon!

A red wolf in the stranglehold of an angel. In striding, your legs jangle like blue ice and a smile full of sorrow and pride has petrified your face and your brow turns pale before the lust of frost;

or it bends silently over the sleep of a watchman who sank down in his wooden shelter.

Frost and smoke. A white shirt of stars burns the carrying shoulders and God's vultures maul your metallic heart.

O the hill of stone. Silent and forgotten, the cool body melts in the silver snow.

Sleep is black. The ear long follows the paths of stars in the ice.

When you awoke, the bells in the village were chiming. Through the east gate, the rosy day made its silvery entrance.

*Song of the One Secluded*

# IN VENICE

Silence in the nightly room.
The candelabrum flickers silver
Before the singing breath
Of the lonely one;
Magical clouds of roses.

A blackish swarm of flies
Darkens the stone room
And the head of the homeless one
Bristles with the agony
Of a golden day.

Night on the motionless sea.
Star and blackish journey
Vanished along the canal.
Child, your sickly smile
Followed me softly in sleep.

# LIMBO

By autumn walls, there shadows
On the hill seek the sounding gold,
Grazing evening clouds
In the calm of withered plane trees.
This age breathes darker tears,
Damnation, when the dreamer's heart
Overflows with purple sunset glow
And the melancholy of a smoking city;
Golden cool wafts from the graveyard
After the striding man, the stranger,
As though a delicate corpse followed in the shadows.

Softly the stone building chimes;
The orphans' garden, the dark almshouse,
A red ship on the canal.
Putrefying men and women
Rise and sink, dreaming in the dark,
And from blackish gates
Angels with cold brows emerge;
Blue, the mothers' lament for the dead.
It rolls through their long hair,
A fiery wheel, the round day
Of earth's endless agony.

In cool, purposeless rooms
Old belongings rot, with bony hands
Unholy childhood gropes in the dark
For fairy tales,
The fat rat gnaws at door and chest,

A heart
Stiffens in snowy silence.
The purple curses of hunger
Echo in the putrid dark,
The black swords of lies,
As though brazen gates were slamming shut.

# THE SUN

Daily the yellow sun comes over the hill.
The forest is lovely, the dark animal,
Man; hunter or herdsman.

Reddish the fish rises in the green pond.
Beneath the round sky
The fisherman glides softly in his blue barge.

Slowly the grape ripens, the wheat.
When the day silently inclines,
Good and evil are prepared.

When night falls,
The wayfarer softly raises heavy eyelids;
The sun breaks from a gloomy gorge.

# SONG OF A CAPTIVE BLACKBIRD

*for Ludwig von Ficker*

Dark breath in green branches.
Small blue flowers float around the face
Of the lonely one, his golden steps
Dying away beneath the olive tree.
Night flutters up on drunken wing.
Humility bleeds so softly,
Dew dripping slowly from the blossoming thorn.
The mercy of radiant arms
Enfolds a breaking heart.

# SUMMER

In the evening the cuckoo's lament
Falls silent in the wood.
The wheat bows lower,
Lower the red poppy.

A black storm threatens
Above the hill.
The cricket's old song
Expires in the field.

The leaves of the chestnut
Never stir.
Your dress rustles
On the winding stair.

Quietly the candle shines
In the dark room;
A silver hand
Put it out;

Wind-free, starless night.

# THE DECLINE OF SUMMER

The green summer has become
So quiet, your crystal countenance.
By the evening pond, the flowers died,
A startled blackbird's cry.

Vain hope of life. Now in the house
The swallow prepares for her journey
And the sun is setting beyond the hill;
Night now beckons for a journey to the stars.

Silence of villages; in all directions
The deserted forests sound. Heart,
Bend more lovingly now
Over the calmly sleeping woman.

The green summer has become
So quiet and the step of the stranger
Chimes through the silver night.
If a blue deer were to think of its path

And the melodious sound of its spiritual years!

# YEAR

Dark silence of childhood. Beneath greening ash trees
Meekness grazes with bluish glance; golden repose.
The scent of violets delights something dark; swaying wheat
In the evening, seeds and the golden shadows of melancholy.
The carpenter is cutting beams; in the twilight vale
The mill grinds; a purple mouth arches in the hazel leaves,
Something male is bending red across silent waters.
Autumn is quiet, the spirit of the forest; a golden cloud
Follows the lonely one, the black shadow of the descendant.
Tilt in a room of stone; beneath old cypress trees
The tears of nightly images collect into a spring;
Golden eye of the beginning, dark patience of the end.

# OCCIDENT

*In homage to Else Lasker-Schüler*

### I

Moon, as if a dead thing emerged
From a blue cave,
And many blossoms fall
Onto the cliff path.
Something ill cries silvery
By the evening pond,
On a black barge
Lovers crossed into death.

Or Elis's steps
Chime through the grove,
The hyacinth grove,
And fade again beneath oaks.
O the boy's form
Shaped by crystal tears
And nightly shadows.
Jagged lightning brightens the brow,
The ever cool one,
When a springtime storm
Sounds by the greening hill.

### 2

The green forests of our homeland
Are so quiet,

The crystal wave
Dying slowly by the crumbling wall
And we have cried in our sleep;
In evening summer, singing people
Walk with hesitant steps
Along the thorny hedge
In the holy calm
Of the vineyard's distant, dying light;
Shadows now in the cool womb
Of night, grieving eagles.
So softly a lunar beam closes
The purple marks of melancholy.


### 3


You great cities
Built of stone
On the plain!
So speechlessly
The homeless one follows
The wind, bare trees by the hill,
With his dark brow.
You streams, dusky in the distance!
The horrid red of sunset
In storm-clouds
Wakes wretched fear.
You dying peoples!
Pale wave
Shattering on the shore of night,
Falling stars.

# SPRINGTIME OF THE SOUL

A sudden cry in sleep; the wind plunges through black alleys,
The blue of springtime waves through snapping branches,
Purple dew of night and the stars all around are going out.
The river dawns in shades of green, silver the ancient
    avenues
And the towers of the town. O gentle drunkenness
On the gliding barge and the blackbird's dark cries
In childlike gardens. Now rosy profusion grows light.

Solemnly the waters burble. O the damp shadows of the
    mead,
The striding beast; things greening, blossoming branches
Touch the crystal brow; shimmering, rocking barge.
Gently the sun sounds in clouds of roses on the hillside.
Great is the fir wood's silence, the serious shadows by the
    river.

Purity! Purity! Where are the terrible paths of death,
Of grey, stony silence, the cliffs of night
And the shades without peace? Luminous abyss of sun.

Sister, when I found you by a secluded glade
In the forest and it was noon and great was the silence of
    beasts;
Pale girl beneath the wild oak, and the thorn bloomed silver.
Immense dying and in my heart a singing flame.

The waters flow darker round the beautiful play of fish.
Hour of sorrow, silent contemplation of the sun;

The soul is a stranger on this earth. Blue darkens
Spiritually above mutilated forest and in the village
A dark bell chimes long; peaceful escort.
Silently the myrtle blooms over the dead man's white
    eyelids.

The waters resound softly in the sinking afternoon
And the shore's wilderness greens darker, joy in the rosy
    wind;
The brother's gentle song by the evening hillside.

# IN DARKNESS

With its silence the soul begets blue springtime.
Beneath damp branches of evening
The lovers' brows sank in shudders.

O the greening cross. In dark conversation
Man and woman recognized one another.
By a blank wall
The lonely one strolls with his constellations.

Above moon-gleamed forest paths
The wilderness of forgotten hunts
Sank down; a glance of blue
Breaks from crumbling cliffs.

# SONG OF THE ONE SECLUDED

*For Karl Borromaeus Heinrich*


Full of harmonies is the flight of birds. The green forests
Have gathered by evening to more silent huts;
The crystal meadows of the deer.
Something dark calms the brook's murmur, the damp
     shadows

And the flowers of summer that chime lovely in the wind.
Already the brow of the pensive man is in twilight.

And the little lamp of goodness shines in his heart
And the peace of his meal; for hallowed are bread and wine
By the hands of God, and your brother looks at you softly
With nightly eyes, that he may rest from thorny travels.
O to dwell in the soulful blue of night.

Lovingly too the room's silence enfolds the shadows of
     the old,
Their purple torments, lament of a great lineage
Which now passes piously in the lonely descendant.

For ever more radiantly the patient sufferer wakens
By the petrified threshold from black minutes of madness,
And the cool blue enfolds him mightily and the luminous
     end of autumn,

The silent house and the legends of the forest,
Measure and law and the lunar paths of the one secluded.

*Dream and Derangement*

In the evening the father became an old man; in dark rooms the mother's face turned to stone and upon the boy lay the curse of his degenerate line. At times he remembered his childhood filled with sickness, dread and darkness, secretive games in the garden of stars, or how he fed rats in the twilit court. From a blue mirror the slim figure of his sister emerged and he fell like a dead man into the dark. At night his mouth broke open like a red fruit and the stars began to gleam above his mute sorrow. His dreams filled the old house of his forefathers. In the evening he liked to walk across the crumbling graveyard, or he went to the twilight chamber of the dead, there to gaze at corpses with the green stains of putrefaction on their beautiful hands. At the monastery gate he asked for a piece of bread; the shadow of a black horse sprang from the dark and startled him. When he lay in his cool bed, he was suddenly overcome by inexpressible tears. But there was no one there to lay a hand on his brow. When autumn came, he walked, a clairvoyant, across brown meadows. O, the hours of wild enchantment, the evenings by the green river, the hunts. O, the soul that gently sang the song of the yellowed reed; fiery piety. Silently and long he gazed into the toad's star eyes, touched the coolness of old stones with shuddering hands and gave voice to the venerable legend of the blue spring. O, the silver fishes and the fruit that fell from stunted trees. The musical chords of his steps filled him with pride and contempt for man. On his way home he came across a deserted castle. Crumbling gods stood in the garden, sorrowing in the evening. Yet it seemed to him: here I have lived forgotten years. An organ chorale filled him with God's shudders. But in a dark cave he passed his days, lied and stole and hid, a flaming wolf, from his mother's white face. O, the hour when with a mouth of stone he sank to earth in the garden of stars and the murderer's shadow came upon him. With a purple brow he entered the moor and the wrath of God chastised his metal shoulders; O, the birches in the storm, the dark beasts that avoided his deranged paths. Hatred burned up his heart, lust, when in the greening summer garden he did violence to the silent child, recognizing in its radiant face his own deranged one. Alas, one evening by the window, when a gruesome skeleton, death came forth from purple flowers. O, you towers and bells; and the shadows of night fell on him like stone.

No one loved him. Lies and vice burned his head in twilight rooms. The blue rustle of a woman's dress turned him into a pillar of stone and in the door stood his mother's nightly form. Above his head reared the shadow of evil. O, you nights and stars. In the evening he walked past the mountain with the cripple; on its icy peak lay the rosy gleam of sunset and his heart chimed softly in the twilight. Heavily the stormy firs sank over them and the red hunter emerged from the forest. When night fell, his heart broke like crystal and darkness beat his brow. Beneath bare oaks he strangled a wild cat with icy hands. To his right appeared the white shape of a lamenting angel, and in the dark the cripple's shadow grew. But this man lifted a stone and threw it at him so he fled wailing, and with a sigh the angel's gentle face faded away in the tree's shadow. Long he lay in a stony field and saw with amazement the golden tent of the stars. Chased by bats he plunged off into the dark. Breathless he entered the crumbling house. A wild animal, he drank from the blue waters of the courtyard's well until he shivered with cold. Feverish he sat on icy steps and raged against God that he would die. O, the grey face of dread when he raised his round eyes above a dove's cut throat. Darting over strange stairs he met a Jewish girl, and he reached for her black hair and he took her mouth. A thing hostile followed him through gloomy alleys and his ear was rent by iron clatter. Along autumn walls he, a young sexton, softly followed the silent priest; beneath withered trees he drunkenly breathed in the scarlet of those venerable robes. O, the crumbling disk of the sun. Sweet torments consumed his flesh. In a desolate house, his bleeding form appeared to him stiff with filth. More deeply he loved the exalted works of stone; the tower that storms the starry blue sky night after night with its hellish grimaces; the cool grave in which man's fiery heart is kept. Woe to the inexpressible guilt this heart proclaims. But when pondering blazing things he walked down the autumn river beneath bare trees, there appeared to him a flaming demon in a coat of hair, his sister. When they awoke, the stars above their heads went out.

O, from the cursed lineage. When in defiled rooms every destiny has been fulfilled, death enters the house with putrid steps. O, if only it were spring outside and a sweet bird were singing in the blossoming tree. But gruesomely the meagre green withers by the window of the nocturnal ones and blood-dripping hearts still plot evil. O, the twilight spring paths of the pensive one. More justly does the blooming hedge delight him, the peasant's young wheat-seed and the singing bird, God's gentle creature; the evening bell and the beautiful community of man. If he might only forget his fate and the thorny sting. Freely the brook becomes green where his foot takes silver steps, and a speaking tree rustles above his deranged head. So he lifts the snake with a frail hand, and his heart melted in fiery tears. Exalted is the silence of the forest, greening dark and the mossy animals that flutter up when night falls. O the shudder when everything is aware of its guilt and walks along thorny paths. Thus he found in the thorn-bush the white form of a child bleeding for the coat of her bridegroom. But buried in his steel hair, he stood before her and suffered mutely. O the radiant angels whom the purple night wind scattered. Long nights he lived in a crystal cave and leprosy grew silver on his brow. A shadow, he walked down the mule-track beneath autumnal stars. Snow fell and blue gloom filled the house. His father's hard voice, like a blind man's, sounded and conjured up dread. Woe to the bowed appearance of women. Beneath petrified hands, fruit and tools decayed before the horrified lineage. A wolf tore the firstborn to pieces and in dark gardens, the sisters fled to skeletal old men. A deranged seer, he sang along crumbling walls and God's wind devoured his voice. O the voluptuousness of death. O you children of a dark lineage. The evil flowers of blood shimmer silver at his temple, the cold moon in his broken eyes. O, the nightly ones; O, the damned.

Deep is the slumber in dark poisons, filled with stars and the mother's white face, her stony face. Death is bitter, the fare of those weighed down by guilt; in the stem's brown branches, earthen faces fell to grinning ruin. But he sang softly in the green shadow of the elder when he awoke from evil dreams; a rosy angel approached him, sweet playmate, so that he, a gentle deer, slumbered by night; and he saw the starry face of purity. The sunflowers sank golden across the garden fence when summer came. O, the diligence of bees and the walnut's green leaves; the passing thunderstorms. The poppy bloomed silver also and bore in its green capsule our nightly star-dreams. O, how silent was the house when his father passed into the dark. The fruit ripened purple on the tree and the gardener kept his hard hands busy; O the signs woven of hair in the radiant sun. But in the evening the shade of the dead man stepped softly into his family's grieving circle and his step sounded like crystal over the greening meadow before the forest. Silently they gathered at the table; dying, they broke the blood-dripping bread with waxen hands. Woe the stony eyes of the sister, when at supper her insanity appeared on her brother's nightly brow, when the mother's bread turned to stone beneath her suffering hands. O the putrefied ones, when they mutely spoke of hell with their silver tongues. Thus the lamps went out in the cool room and suffering people looked at each other in silence from behind purple masks. Rain murmured all night long and refreshed the lea. In thorny wilderness, the dark one followed faded paths in the wheat, the song of the lark and the gentle silence of green branches, that he might find peace. O, you villages and mossy steps, glowing sight. But like bones the footsteps stagger over snakes asleep at the edge of the forest and the ear always follows the vulture's raging shriek. Stony wasteland he found at evening, a dead man's escort into his father's dark house. A purple cloud darkened his head until he silently attacked his own blood and image, a lunar face; sank into the void like a stone, for in the broken mirror, a dying youth, the sister appeared; night devoured the cursed line.

# Publications in *"Der Brenner"*

## 1914–1915

# IN HELLBRUNN

Following again the blue lament of evening
Along the hill, along the springtime pond –
As if above it the shades of those long dead hovered,
The shades of prelates, of noble women –
Their flowers bloom already, sombre violets
In the evening vale, the blue spring's
Crystal wave murmurs. The oaks grow green
So sacredly over the dead's forgotten paths,
The golden cloud above the pond.

# THE HEART

The wild heart grew white by the wood;
O dark fear
Of death, when gold
Died in a grey cloud.
November evening.
By the bare gate of the slaughterhouse
Stood a cluster of poor women;
Into every basket
Putrid meat fell, and entrails;
Cursed fare!

Evening's blue dove
Did not bring conciliation,
Dark trumpet call
Passed through the elms'
Wet golden leaves,
A torn flag
Steaming with blood,
So that a man listens
In wild dejection.
O! you brazen times
Buried there in the sunset glow.

From a dark hall
The golden form
Of a young woman emerged
Surrounded by pale moons,

Autumnal retinue,
By broken black firs
In the night storm,
The steep citadel.
O heart
Shimmering across into snowy cool.

## SLEEP

Curse you, dark poisons,
White sleep!
This weirdest garden
Of twilight trees
Filled with snakes, moths,
Spiders, bats.
Stranger! Your lost shadow
In the sunset glow,
A gloomy corsair
In the salty sea of misery.
White birds rise at night's edge
Above plummeting cities
Of steel.

# THE THUNDERSTORM

You wild mountains, exalted sorrow
Of eagles.
Golden clouds
Smoke above stony wasteland.
The pines breathe patient repose,
Black lambs by the abyss,
Where suddenly the blue
Is strangely mute,
The gentle hum of bumble-bees.
O green flower –
O silence.

Dreamlike, the torrent's dark spirits
Make the heart tremble,
Darkness
That descends upon chasms!
White voices
Straying through horrible courtyards,
Torn terraces,
The fathers' immense rancour, the lament
Of the mothers,
The boy's golden war cry
And something not yet born
Sighing from blind eyes.

O pain, you flaming vision
Of the great soul!
There in the black throng
Of steeds and wagons

A rose-horrid lightning bolt
Flashes into the sounding spruce.
Magnetic cool
Floats around this proud head,
Burning melancholy
Of an angry god.

Fear, you poisonous snake,
Black one, die among stones!
Then the wild torrents
Of tears gush,
Storm-compassion,
The snowy peaks all around
Echo in threatening thunder.
Fire
Purifies the torn night.

# EVENING

With figures of dead heroes,
Moon, you fill
The silent forests,
Crescent moon –
With the gentle embrace
Of lovers
The shadows of illustrious times,
The rotting cliffs all round;
Such a bluish glow
In the direction of town,
Where cold and evil
A putrid lineage lives,
Preparing a dark future
For its pale descendants.
You moon-entwined shadows
Sighing deeply in the empty crystal
Of the mountain lake.

# NIGHT

You I sing, wild crags and fissures,
Mountains towering high
In the tempest of night;
You grey towers
Overflowing with infernal sneers,
Blazing animals,
Coarse ferns, firs,
Crystal flowers.
Unending agony,
That you hunted God down
Gentle spirit,
Sighing deeply in plunging waters,
In surging pines.

The fires of peoples
Flame golden all around.
Over blackish cliffs
The wind's glowing bride
Plunges drunken with death,
The blue wave
Of the glacier
And the bell in the valley
Booms mightily:
Flames, curses,
And the dark
Games of lust,
A petrified head
Storms the sky.

# MELANCHOLY

You are immense, dark mouth,
Inside, form shaped
By autumn clouds,
By golden evening calm,
A greenish dusky mountain stream
In the shadow district
Of shattered pines;
A village
That dies piously in brown images.

There the black horses leap
On a foggy pasture.
You soldiers!
From the hill where the dying sun rolls
The laughing blood plunges –
Beneath oaks
Speechless! O resentful melancholy
Of the army; a radiant helmet
Sank clattering from purple brow.

The cool autumn night comes,
Is suddenly alight with stars
Above the shattered bones of men
The quiet female monk.

# THE RETURN

Cyclopean stone retains
The cool of dark years,
Pain and hope,
Unpeopled mountains,
Autumn's golden breath,
Evening cloud –
Purity!

From blue eyes,
Crystal childhood gazes;
Beneath dark firs
Love, hope,
So dew drips from fiery eyelids
Into the stiff grass –
Unstoppable!

O! there the golden footbridge
Shattering in the snow
Of the abyss!
The nightly valley breathes
Blue cool,
Faith, hope!
Greetings, lonely graveyard!

# LAMENT

Youth, from your crystal mouth
Your golden gaze sank to the valley;
The forest wave, red and sallow
In the pitch-black hour of evening.
Evening cuts such a deep wound!

Fear! death's dream complaint,
Withered grave and even the year
Looks out from tree and deer;
Barren field and open soil.
The shepherd calls the fearful flock.

Sister, your blue eyebrows
Softly gesture in the night.
The organ sighs and hell laughs
And shudders befall the heart;
It wants to see angels and stars.

Mother must fear for her small child;
In the shaft, the ore sounds red,
Lust, tears, stony pain,
The dark legends of the Titans.
Melancholy! eagles mourn alone.

# SURRENDER TO NIGHT

Female monk! enfold me in your dark,
You mountains cool and blue!
Dark dew is bleeding down;
The cross looms amid twinkling stars.

Both mouth and lies broke purple
In a cool and crumbling room;
A smile still glows, golden chime,
A bell's dying sounds.

Moon cloud! Wild fruit falls
Blackish from trees at night
And space becomes a grave
And earth's pilgrimage a dream.

## IN THE EAST

The people's dark anger resembles
The wild organ-pipes of winter storms,
The purple wave of combat,
Of defoliated stars.

With shattered brows, silver arms,
Night waves to dying soldiers.
In the shade of the autumn ash
The spirits of the slain sigh.

Thorny wilderness girds the city.
The moon chases terrified women
From bleeding steps.
Wild wolves broke through the gate.

# LAMENT

Sleep and death, the dark eagles
Surge round this head nightlong:
The icy wave of eternity
Would devour the golden image
Of man. On horrifying reefs
His purple body is shattered
And the dark voice laments
Above the sea.
Sister of stormy melancholy
See a fearful barge sinks
Beneath stars,
The silent countenance of night.

# GRODEK

At evening the autumnal forests resound
With deadly weapons, the golden plains
And blue lakes, above them the sun
Rolls more darkly by; night enfolds
The dying warriors, the wild lament
Of their broken mouths.
But in the grassy vale the spilled blood,
Red clouds in which an angry god lives,
Gathers softly, lunar coldness;
All roads lead to black decay.
Beneath the golden boughs of night and stars
The sister's shadow reels through the silent grove
To greet the ghosts of heroes, their bleeding heads;
And the dark flutes of autumn sound softly in the reeds.
O prouder sorrow! you brazen altars
Today an immense anguish feeds the mind's hot flame,
The unborn descendants.

# REVELATION AND DESTRUCTION

Strange are the nightly paths of man. When I sleepwalked past rooms of stone and a quiet little lamp stood burning in each one, a copper candelabrum, and when I sank shivering onto my bed, the black shadow of the female stranger stood at my head and silently I hid my face in my slow hands. And the hyacinth had just opened its blue blossoms at the window and the old prayer sprang to the breathing one's purple lip, crystal tears sank from his eyelids, crying for the world's bitterness. At this hour I was the pale son in my father's death. In blue shudders the night wind came down from the hill, the dark lament of the mother, dying again, and I saw the black hell in my heart; a minute of shimmering silence. Softly an inexpressible face – a dying young man – emerged from the chalky wall, the beauty of a lineage returning home. Moon-white the cool of stone enfolded the wakeful brow, the steps of the shades died away on crumbling stairs, a rosy round-dance in the little garden.

Silent I sat and lonely, drinking wine in a deserted tavern beneath smoky wooden beams; a radiant corpse bending over a dark thing and a dead lamb lay at my feet. From putrid blue the sister's pale form emerged and thus did her bleeding mouth speak: Pierce, black thorn. Woe, even now my silver arms are sounding with wild storms and thunder. Flow, blood, from the lunar feet, blooming on nightly paths where the rat darts screaming. Flame up, you stars in my arched eyebrows; and the heart rings softly in the night. A red shade broke into the house with flaming sword, fled with snowy brow. O bitter death.

And a dark voice spoke from within me: I broke my black steed's neck in the nightly wood, for madness was leaping from his purple eyes; the shade of the elms fell upon me, the spring's blue laughter and the black cool of night, when I, a wild hunter, roused a snowy deer; in a hell of stone my countenance died.

And a drop of blood fell shimmering into the lonely one's wine; and when I drank of it, it tasted more bitter than poppy; and a blackish cloud enveloped my head, the crystal tears of damned angels; and softly blood poured from the sister's silver wound and a fiery rain fell upon me.

At the forest's edge I wish to walk, a silent thing from whose mute hands the sun of hair sank; a stranger by the evening hill who weeping raises his eyelids above the city of stone; a deer that stands still in the peace of the old elder; O restlessly the twilight head listens, or hesitant steps follow the blue cloud on the hill, and the serious constellations. The green crops softly lead aside, the deer a shy escort on mossy forest paths. The huts of the villagers have mutely withdrawn and in a black lull the blue lament of the mountain torrent terrifies.

But when I descended the cliff path I was overwhelmed by madness and I screamed loudly in the night; and when I bent over the silent waters with silver fingers I saw my countenance had deserted me. And the white voice spoke to me: Kill yourself! Sighing, a boy's shade arose in me and looked at me radiantly with crystal eyes, so I sank weeping beneath the trees, the immense vault of stars.

Restless journey through wild rocks far from evening hamlets, flocks returning home; far away the sinking sun grazes on a crystal meadow and its wild song is unsettling, the bird's lonely cry dying in blue calm. But softly you come in the night while I lay awake on the hill, or raging in a spring storm; and blacker and blacker melancholy clouds the departed head, horrifying flashes of lightning frighten the nightly soul, your hands tear open my breathless chest.

When I went down to the twilight garden and the black shape of evil had left me, I was enfolded by the hyacinth silence of night; and I sailed on a curved barge over the resting pond and sweet peace brushed my petrified brow. Mutely I lay beneath the old willows and the blue sky was far above me and full of stars; and as I lay there gazing and slowly dying, fear and my deepest pain died within me; and the blue shade of the boy rose radiant in the dark, a gentle song; rose on lunar wings over the greening treetops, crystal cliffs the sister's white countenance.

With silver soles I descended the thorny steps and I went into the lime-washed chamber. Softly a candelabrum shone inside and silently I hid my head in purple linen; and the earth cast out a childlike corpse, a lunar thing that emerged slowly from my shadow and sank down stone lintels with shattered arms, flocculent snow.